Featherstone

Alistair Bryce-Clegg

GET THEM TALKING
GET THEM LEARNING

F   iality talk experiences
                         to enhance learning

D1340938

Published 2012 by Featherstone Education
Bloomsbury Publishing plc
50 Bedford Square, London, WC1B 3DP
www.bloomsbury.com

ISBN 978-1-4081-6393-1

Text © Alistair Bryce-Clegg 2012
Design © Lynda Murray
Photographs © Fiona Bryce-Clegg, Shutterstock and London Early Years Foundation/
Emli Bendixen

A CIP record for this publication is available from the British Library.
All rights reserved. No part of this publication may be reproduced
in any form or by any means – graphic, electronic, or mechanical, including
photocopying, recording, taping or information storage or retrieval systems –
without the prior permission in writing of the publishers.

Printed in Great Britain by Latimer Trend & Company Ltd

10 9 8 7 6 5 4 3 2 1

This book is produced using paper that is made from wood grown in
managed, sustainable forests. It is natural, renewable and recyclable.
The logging and manufacturing processes conform to the environmental
regulations of the country of origin.

To see our full range of titles visit **www.bloomsbury.com**

Acknowledgements
Photographs with kind permission of:
London Early Years Foundation
Acorn Childcare Ltd.
Moor Park Primary School (Blackpool)
Claremont Primary School (Blackpool)
Middlefield Primary School (Speke)
The Friars Primary School (Salford)
St Thomas More's Catholic Primary School (Hampshire)
Noah's Ark Pre-School (Hampshire)
Little 1's Day Nursery (Hampshire)
Crofton Hammond Infant's School (Hampshire)
Elizabeth Knowles, Sharon Mordecai and the Hampshire LFSP initiative.

NORWICH CITY COLLEGE
Stock No. A 301265
649.68 BRY
12   Proc   3wk

Contents

Introduction

Ever since I was a little boy I have been fascinated by talk. Not only in the doing of it, but also in the listening to it. Often as a child I could be found listening in on other people's conversations in shops or on buses, much to the embarrassment of my mother! I have always been a sucker for a good story and I was a late developer where reading was concerned so listening to other people 'talking' their stories was perfect. Everything from the mundane routines of their daily lives to their tales of joy, woe and family history – I couldn't get enough.

When I was little and listening in, talking was just talking. I didn't categorize what I was hearing into types of talk, I just knew I liked stories the best. The reason I loved a story? Probably because a good story is often rich in language. Telling a tale allows you to use language that reading out your shopping list doesn't. The best stories are told by people with the widest selection of vocabulary to choose from. The more you know, the more you can say and the more ways you can say it.

Command of language and talk is the single most important thing that we can teach our children. The more that they understand, the more diverse their use of language can be. As talk is so important, it never fails to surprise me that its essential elements are often misunderstood and that quality opportunities for its practice and use rank so low in the learning opportunities that we provide for our children.

There is a long history in teaching of 'adult-led' talk sessions where the adult spends a great deal of time instructing and children only really get a chance to talk when they are responding to adult questioning. This significantly stifles children's opportunities to develop their language skills and also mars their interest and engagement in learning. Even though the Early Years curriculum is far less prescriptive than that of Key Stages One and Two and offers more opportunities than anywhere else in the primary curriculum for children to engage in talk and exploration of language, adult-focused sessions are still very centred around adults speaking and children listening. When I talk to practitioners about why they run their Early Years teaching sessions like this, they talk about a 'top down' pressure: an expectation that often comes from management

who have little or no experience of Foundation Stage. Some staff have also told me about their own insecurities and lack of knowledge and confidence for how to deliver their teaching in any other way. If we are going to change the ingrained practice of 'chalk and talk' to allow children the opportunity to engage with their learning in a meaningful and personal way, then there needs to be a huge pedagogical shift not only from practitioners but their management teams and the institutions that are responsible for delivering the training that prepares adults to be effective practitioners in Early Years.

In this book I have outlined some of the types of talk that commonly occur in our everyday interactions, although the list is by no means exhaustive! I have described the common obstacles that can prevent opportunities for these types of talk to occur as well as ideas for how you can support their development. Each section also includes a short case study, 'A day in the life of ABC', which is taken from my practice as a consultant in a variety of settings.

Although on occasion, many of us feel the need to talk to ourselves, talk is usually at least a two-way process where we take it in turns to both contribute and listen. Not only do we have to think about what we are going to say, how we are going to say it and select the appropriate vocabulary to say it with, in a conversation we also have to listen to the thoughts of others. What they say and how they say it will ultimately affect our contribution to the conversation and may require us to re-think our original ideas. To talk in a conversation is a complex process that requires children to engage in sustained and shared thinking and communication. It is a fantastic forum for a plethora of skill development.

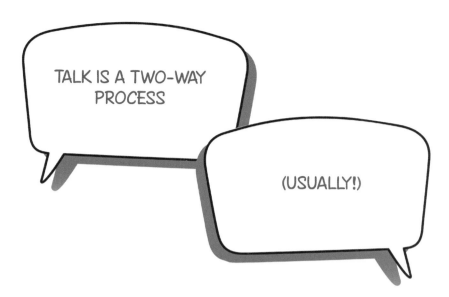

TALK IS A TWO-WAY PROCESS

(USUALLY!)

As Early Years practitioners we need to regularly engage our children in a variety of types of extended talk including narratives, explanations, pretend talk and other forms of complex conversations. It may sound a little strange but an Early Years environment can also present the greatest opportunity for quality talk to get lost. I am sure in every setting there is lots of talking going on between children and their significant adults and peers, but what sort of talk is it? Does it require children to think before engaging in the dialogue? Are adults recognizing the opportunities to actively listen, assess and engage in a way that will help to take children's development further? Often the talk from adults tends to be instructional, telling children that it is 'time to....', or requesting that they 'go and....'. Although this is a type of talk, it is not the type of talk that is going to inspire learning. It is the type of talk that we use to facilitate order and control. Undoubtedly this is a necessary part of any classroom or setting, but the primary role of the adult should be to listen, assess and then scaffold learning into the child's play.

We need to see talk as a two-way enquiry, where both talker and listener use the information they are receiving and the information they have already got stored in their brain to find meaning in what is being said. Once they have identified the meaning, then they have to use everything they have available to them to construct a response. All of the above takes brain power and time, especially if it is a bit new to you. One of the essential elements of supporting a child in their talk development is to give them time – time to think and time to answer. We need to create a 'thinking time' culture where children genuinely feel that they have time to think and not that the adult is 'waiting for an answer'. If a child feels under pressure, then they are less able to think clearly because they are too busy worrying about thinking of the right answer as quickly as possible.

Often using another child or adult as a 'talk partner' can alleviate some of this stress and expectation. The process of articulating thoughts helps to sort and re-sort them. Also the views of others can help to clarify or challenge thinking. One of the issues that can arise in Early Years with the introduction of a talk partner is that at this stage in their development children are not familiar with having to listen to the views of others. It can end up with one child who does all of the talking and dominates the discussion, or children who disagree but haven't got the language to be able to resolve that disagreement or offer up a solution. Adults have to model appropriate behaviours and strategies as well as create lots of opportunities for those strategies to be practised.

Chapter 1

The reluctant talker

Although some children seem to talk constantly, others seem reluctant to talk and are not as expressive. They do not seem to be prepared to talk in order to express their needs; they rarely ask questions or share their opinions. They will only access activities that do not require them to use a lot of talk. Being quiet in new situations is very common in young children. This is a normal part of growing up and, once a situation, adult or setting becomes familiar to them, they lose that initial shyness.

Why it generally happens

New situations often have a profound effect on young children's well-being. Their anxiety levels are significantly raised and so they revert back more towards 'flight or fight' mode, as opposed to being relaxed and open. When children first arrive at a setting everything is new: the space, the resources, the people, the routines. It will take some of them quite a while to feel secure enough to find their voice.

What it is like for the child

Starting at a setting is a bit like you starting a brand new job in a brand new place with a brand new set of adults. You have no idea what anyone's name is, where anything is kept, whether the people you are with are nice or not. There is so much for you to think about that you are not likely to be completely yourself on the first day – or even for the first month. For some children, starting at your setting is just like that but worse as they do not have as many (if any) of the well-developed social skills that you and I have got. Nor do they have the past experience that tells them that, even though it is a bit scary now, it will all become familiar very quickly. They also don't have our strategies for what to do if something goes wrong, and that will worry them because their significant adult isn't there to sort it all out. It is little wonder they are quiet!

How you can help the reluctant talker?

◆ Follow the child's lead. You may notice that the child is more talkative during certain tasks or activities where they feel comfortable and some elements of the task are familiar. Provide frequent opportunities for the child to engage in these activities.

◆ Provide extra time for the child to produce a response. If it is whispered, accept the response as a good start. Indicate that you are having some trouble hearing and suggest that the problem is yours: "I didn't quite catch that. I must be having trouble with my ears."

◆ Act as though they did speak and respond to the unspoken remark. For example, if you give them something and say, "Say thank you", then continue, "You're welcome", just as if they had said "Thank you". (This is not meant to be sarcastic. You are modelling appropriate conversation to encourage talking.)

◆ Encourage guessing. It takes the right/wrong edge off the response. Say, for example, "Guess what we are having for dinner."

◆ Model good speech while the child is busy with an activity. Talk about what they are doing and the items they are using. There is no expectation of a response but the child hears the words and sentences that match the activity.

◆ Reward speech efforts immediately. Praise from an adult is a very powerful reward!

◆ Never try to force a reluctant talker to talk or try to 'catch them out'. This will only raise the child's anxiety further and make the problem significantly worse.

Children can be reluctant talkers for a variety of reasons. Sometimes those reasons are just related to settling in, but sometimes they are far more deep-rooted and require careful and sensitive handling. It is important to know that this is not a case of 'will not talk' but 'cannot talk' because of fear. In these instances you need to seek some professional help and advice as to how you can best support that child in overcoming their anxiety.

Chapter 2

An environment for talk

To help our children to become effective talkers we first have to make sure that we have created a learning environment that supports and enriches that talk development. It is true that talk at its most basic level is made up of thoughts turned into words that come out of the mouth, but there are a number of different types of talk that require different sorts of experiences and different vocabulary.

Developing a 'talk-rich' environment

A 'talk-rich' environment is one where the children's level of talk and vocabulary are accurately assessed and opportunities are created for further development and enhancement both indoors and out. Although talk is everywhere in an early years setting, it is good to identify the areas you have got that lend themselves to particular types of talk development. For example, where in your setting are there most opportunities to develop talk for turn taking and negotiation? Where are there most opportunities for developing talk for empathy and understanding? Knowing the different types of talk that you would like to develop will help you to create and resource areas that will support the children with their learning.

Children also need different sorts of spaces to develop different types of talk, from tiny private den-like spaces to great big open outdoor spaces. They need spaces to whisper, spaces to shout, spaces to talk to a significant other, spaces to chat with friends, and spaces to address a larger group.

Different children's talk will develop at different rates and their specific needs for talk development will be different, so it is important that you use your observation and assessment information to help you to plan for which areas you are going to create and also their size and shape. Can you match your environment layout to your last assessments and observations?

When you are thinking about spaces to encourage talk you may not want to (or have the room) to create big areas that use lots of floor space. If that is the case then you can create small areas in different parts of your learning environment both indoors and out.

In all of your spaces you want to provide lots of interesting open-ended resources that will appeal to different children in different ways and inspire them to want to talk. You can also provide specific resources that are aimed at developing a specific element of talk. For example, when you are looking at developing the language of turn taking, you should provide activities and games that need children to be able to acquire and use that language before they can take part.

If you know that the children you are working with have little or no language for the talk you are trying to develop, then the adult plays a key role in modelling and supporting the introduction and use of the type of talk. Once the children start to become familiar with using the talk then they need lots of opportunities to practise it.

Conflict resolution

When it comes to types of talk, like talk for conflict resolution, this tends to come up as part of children's everyday play and interaction; for example, when something has gone wrong such as someone taking an extra turn on the bike.

As adults we often get caught up in the drama of the situation and provide a 'quick fix' resolution to the problem. What we don't do (often because of time) is to discuss options and possibilities for an effective resolution in a way that a child might be able to comprehend and understand. For some adults, compromise is an alien concept. It is usually ten times worse for children! If it is a particular issue for any children in your setting then you might want to think about planning activities that require the children taking part to have to compromise and use their talk skills to resolve any conflict however major or minor.

To be able to compromise, children have to first be able to feel some empathy for the person that they are going to have to compromise with. So if conflict resolution is an issue don't wade straight in with high tension conflict activities that will more than likely end up with one of the children giving the other a slap (because they don't have the language or skills to communicate efficiently)! Start by creating talk activities that are based around empathy. If possible take the 'personal' element out of it so that you are not re-enacting a real event that has already happened involving the children that you are working with. This will only serve to raise their stress levels and remind them of how angry they were.

Create role-play or small-world situations where children can translate their thoughts and feelings through other characters. That way they do not feel inhibited, embarrassed or judged and are more likely to be receptive to the play. Children will often use fantasy, small-world and role-play situations to practise and rehearse their talk, either revisiting actual experiences and replaying them through role-play or creating an imaginary situation and talking their way through it.

Role-play

When it comes to role-play, how big your role-play area is and the resources that you have in it are of paramount importance. There is no point saying that you want to develop children's talk using role-play and then having a tiny area that only three children can fit into!

The key to effective role-play for language development is the ambiguity of the core resources that are in it. If we over-theme our role-play space then we are stifling the children's ability to consolidate and enhance their vocabulary and use of language. In addition, to role-play anything, the children have to have some understanding of what they are going to role-play – otherwise how will they know what they are supposed to do?

It is worth remembering that a cardboard box is never just a cardboard box when it is in the play of a child with even just a little bit of imagination. Whereas a postbox is a postbox, unless it is in the play of a child with a very vivid imagination. Therefore, keep your 'core' role-play resourcing simple and un-themed; for example, cardboard boxes, tubes, crates, fabric and den-making materials. Then enhance it with 'real' objects that you have collected to support a theme or interest.

This setting had a 'deconstructed' role-play offering open-ended talk opportunities. These children are using an enhancement box that has been themed around an interest in the hairdresser's. Once these children have left the role-play the hairdresser play might continue or be turned into something completely different, depending on the knowledge, needs and preferences of the children who replace them. To ensure really effective talk development your role-play should allow this level of flexibility.

Once you have set up an open-ended provision for role-play in your setting, then you need to be strategic in how you are using that provision to meet the specific talk needs of your children and to develop their skills.

To help you to do this you should plan the specific skills that you are going to focus on across a given period of time and then resource the play to support that skill development. So, instead of planning to create a post office, which everyone will have to play in whether the post office is relevant or interesting or not, you should plan to develop a talk skill that can be applied wherever the children's imaginations take their play.

Here are the sorts of talking skills you should consider in your early years setting:

* Talk for social interaction – **building relationships through cooperation, taking turns, joining in and sharing.**

* Talk for making choices and decisions **– developing curiosity and questioning ideas.**

* Talk for increasing language development **– using familiar and newly introduced vocabulary in different contexts.**

* Talk for communication **– developing conversation, listening and responding.**

* Talk for expressing emotions **– being able to talk about both positive and negative feelings.**

* Talk for recalling own experiences **– expressing what they have just done to another person.**

* Talk for developing mathematical language and concepts in a meaningful context.

* Talk for day-to-day activities **– including things they do at home and those they do in the early years setting.**

* Talk for expressing ideas **– for example, in the construction of props.**

* Talk for projecting themselves into the feelings and actions of others **– in both real and imaginary instances, such as fantasy characters from TV, fairy and folk tales.**

* Talk for taking on a role in a given situations **– in both real and fantasy instances.**

* Talk for conflict resolution **– using the language of compromise and negotiation.**

* Talk for problem-solving and organization **– this is helpful for many situations, for example, tidying up!**

Small-world play

Providing flexible and open-ended resources to develop dramatic play is not just confined to your role-play area. Plain wooden bricks used in small-world play can have the same effect, only in miniature. A toy pig is always a pig and a toy car is always a car; but a small plain wooden brick can be a hundred different things depending on the child's imagination.

Play indoors and outside can be two very different things, and the same applies to talk in small-world play. We need to make sure that our small-world play is not just resigned to the carpet area or the farm, but that we give opportunities for children to play with their small-world resources outdoors in 'real' environments full of 'real' objects that will not only provide a setting for their play but will also support them in the development of their language for the real things that they can see, hear, smell and touch.

In the same way that you would plan for a skill development in role-play, you should do the same for your small-world sessions.

Here are examples of some of the talk skills that you might plan to support through small-world play:

- Talk for size comparison and properties – **using a variety of small-world resources.**

- Talk for cooperation and collaboration – **beginning to work as part of a group.**

- Talk for sharing and turn taking – **playing with the small-world resources with another child.**

- Talk for the exploration of role-play – **using small-world characters.**

- Talk for the naming of familiar objects and animals – **developing language using specfied small-world resources.**

- Talk for descriptive language – **developing language through chosen small-world items.**

- Talk for positional language – **using the small-world resources to develop an understanding of relative position.**

- Talk for naming attributes of common objects and animals.

- Talk for developing an awareness of a real-life environment – **both their own and those that are different from their own.**

- Talk for communicating emotions – **for example fear and joy.**

- Talk for discussion of previous experiences – **developing language to describe both good and bad experiences.**

- Talk for description and exploration – **developing the language of colour, texture, shape and size of objects found in real and imaginary habitats.**

- Talk for awareness of danger.

- Talk for the recognition of 'sameness' and 'difference'

- Talk for finding out about past events – **in their own lives and the lives of others.**

- Talk for making choices – **using a selection of small-world resources.**

- Talk for organizing ideas and experiences.

Of course, quality talk development is not restricted to role-play and small-world activities. There are opportunities for talk development in every area; it is just that some lend themselves to the enhancement of particular types of talk more than others.

I have created a list of some of the types of talk that we should be working on with children. It is by no means exhaustive; but it should give you an overview of what you need to develop, what might hinder that development and what you can do to help.

Chapter 3

Talk for turn taking

Being able to take turns while talking is just as important as being able to use talk to allow you to take turns. Any conversation (other than with yourself or the wall!) requires each participant to take turns at both speaking and listening, so the concept of being able to take 'a talking turn' is fundamental to carrying out a conversation.

In early education, lots of children struggle with being able to wait or take their turn. When they are young, life is very 'immediate' and it is hard for them to understand why they can't have what they want exactly when they want it (which is usually 'now'). So working with children on developing their turn taking is two-fold: turn taking in talk and talk for turn taking.

Waiting to talk

Being able to listen and judge when it is appropriate to speak is not only important in terms of understanding, but interrupting or talking over someone is regarded by society as rude. Learning to take turns is also about learning important social expectations. As practitioners, though, it is important to remember that young children do not have an automatic 'stop valve' that prevents their thoughts from gushing out of their mouths and that having to wait can be very frustrating. In the early stages of development, children assume that all life revolves around them. Why wouldn't everyone want to hear what they have got to say as soon as they realize that they want to say it?

We need to enable children to understand the necessity of waiting. This can be achieved by helping them to acknowledge how they feel when someone interrupts them or they are prevented from speaking. The best way to get understanding is to create an awareness of empathy for others – but this in itself is easier said than done. This isn't something that is going to happen over night and for some children will not happen as a matter of course, which is why it is important that it is recognized as a feature of children's talk development and that opportunities to nurture it are actively built into planning, environment and teaching.

> By waiting your turn to speak and avoiding interrupting another person, you not only show your desire to work together with the other members of your society, you also show respect for your fellow members.
>
> **Rita Cook,** *The Complete Guide to Robert's Rules of Order Made Easy*, **Atlantic Publishing, 2008**

There are some things that might obstruct learning to talk for turn taking:

◆ **Lack of opportunities** – many children enjoy solo play activities because they don't require sharing; they can play their game to their rules and their own agenda.

◆ **Too many resources** – at home children will often have a wide selection of toys to play with or engage in activities that don't require them to take turns, like watching their own television in their own room.

◆ **The wrong type of conversations** – conversations can be a help or a hindrance when it comes to turn taking. It depends on how they are conducted: conversations that do not require or allow a response are not going to help to develop children's skills!

◆ **Not enough language** – alongside mastering how conversation works and perfecting the ability to keep the thought inside their head until it is their turn to speak (this often takes a LONG time and a great deal of practice!), children need to understand the 'language' of turn taking and negotiation. They can only do this through modelling and practice.

◆ **Too much talking** – adults can often talk for too long or at an inappropriate level which causes children to lose interest and switch off.

There are some things that you can do to help children develop their talk for turn taking:

◆ **Talk one to one** – create lots of opportunities to talk to children on a one-to-one basis. Make turn taking the focus for talking. Keep your interactions short to start with and focus on a subject that the children will engage with. Remind the children about what you are looking for and how they might achieve it; then give them opportunities to practise, practise, practise.

◆ **Board games** – stock your setting with interesting games that require children to take turns to be able to play. Make sure that you have a variety of games for two players to multiple players. Also make sure that the children are really familiar with how to play the games before you leave them out as part of your continuous provision.

◆ **Talk games** – play lots and lots of oral games that involve children taking turns. Keep them simple and short to start with: no one likes to have to wait for their turn! Games where children have to listen before being able to take their turn are especially good for developing this skill. These could be games like 'I went to the shop and I bought…' where each player repeats the list and adds on a new item.

There are lots of opportunities to encourage children to take turns in almost every aspect of learning in the Early Years learning environment. If you offer a very structured task or play experience to children then the options of what they can do are limited by the structure in place. This can sometimes restrict or even take away children's need to discuss and negotiate with each other. Remove this structure and replace it with open ended resources and you immediately create an opportunity for discussion and negotiation. In the examples on the following pages, this is exactly what I did with role-play.

A day in the life of ABC

Anyone who has heard me speak knows that this type of role-playing activity is a great passion of mine when it comes to developing language, imagination and play. I was first inspired to develop the activity after listening to Pat Broadhead talk about a 'whatever you want it to be area'. I now recommend this style of role-play wherever I go and everyone says it produces brilliant results.

The idea
It is quite simple really. Traditional role-play is very adult directed and over-themed. We might set up a café, Goldilock's house or the veterinary surgery in our role-play area. When there is an adult leading the play, using the language and acting out scenarios, then the children can easily access the experience: the adult facilitates their play. But, when there is no adult, the children have to rely on their own life experience to provide them with the tools that they need to be able to play in that particular environment. How many of the children that we work with have ever been in the operating theatre of a vet, or even ordering their lunch in a café? As adults we have a lot of experience to draw on when it comes to using our imagination. You could say that you have never been to the moon; but you could still imagine what it might be like to be there. That is because you have amassed lots of information throughout your life that your brain can use for reference. Not many EYFS children have that!

So...
You create a space that is full of things that can be anything. It is like that old saying about children getting expensive toys for Christmas and then playing with the box. There is a good reason for that. A toy is a toy, but a box has a million possibilities.

How does it work?
First, I have to warn you it doesn't look 'pretty'! It is, essentially, a pile of boxes, fabric, tubes and crates. The more the children use it the shabbier it will look. But, the level of imagination and language that you will get will be reward enough.

The space can change almost by the minute depending on who is playing in it and, better than that, you can often have multiple role-play scenarios all happening at once based on what the children want to play.

Enhancement
Over time you will create theme or enhancement boxes. These are boxes full of goodies that are linked to a particular child-led interest or theme/topic. When there is an adult leading the play they can use them as a teaching tool. When they leave the play the enhancements are available to the children to either copy the theme of the adult or use in their own non-related play.

Below is an enhancement basket I set up in a setting after one of the children had a new baby brother. We also added books on the subject once we had read them to the children.

Costumes
I always provide lots of fabric in the enhancement boxes. It is good for creating dens and dressing up. Making costumes is a great activity: when I have a tabard with 'police' written across the front I am a policeman, whereas a length of fabric has many, many uses.

Backing paper

Leave out cream or black backing paper with lots of mark-making tools. Children LOVE creating their own drawings that are personal to their individual play scenarios. I take photos of the children drawing, then photos of them using their drawings in play. Then, when the backing sheet is completely full of doodles, we use it as a display of mark making, adding the photos next to the drawings with a bit of annotation about the development of talk/mark making/fine motor skills and so on.

Next job — string up the washing line (at child height as they need to access it most).

Here is one I made today!

I was back in Blackpool today putting together the beginnings of a deconstructed role-play. It will, of course, develop as the staff and children get used to it!

This is the space before we started.

We replaced the old kitchen units with open shelves to house our enhancement boxes and stretched the line from the unit to the wall. We strung another line across the back wall (to the right of the picture).

First we needed to clear the area and then establish where we wanted to have the main den-making space. Empowering children with the ability to be able to dress the environment and change it quickly, as their play changes, is essential. So it needs to be kept simple.

My secret weapon? Camping washing line! It is cheap, flexible and does the job brilliantly. I get mine from Ebay for about £3 a length. It is strong elastic, covered in cotton and then twisted with a hook on either end. There is no need for pegs or knots when making dens with this washing line; you just poke the fabric into a twist and it is gripped there until it is pulled out! Genius.

Then we brought in the boxes. I got some really big ones from a DIY store and Claire (one of the teachers) had a friend who was having a kitchen fitted. Perfect!

A quick master class in using the washing line with pieces of fabric... and then let them get creative!

Oh, and did I mention the opportunities for mark making? Claire has put her backing paper on to the heaters. It worked really well.

Chapter 4

Talk for thinking

There are lots of ways that we can use talk to develop the ways in which children think. We want our children to be curious about the world around them. We can prompt that curiosity by asking them interesting questions that will encourage them to think about their answer rather than just saying 'yes' or 'no'.

It is good to get children to recognize the power of collaborative thinking and to understand that great ideas and effective solutions often come from talking about thoughts and ideas with other people. Often in life it is necessary to explain our thinking, to give reasons and produce evidence for why something has happened or might happen. We can encourage critical thinking in children by asking them very open questions about who, what and why?

Good problem-solving skills are a mixture of all the above, plus the ability to be creative in thinking. Children need opportunities to discuss exciting ideas and have the chance to build on their own ideas and the ideas of others. These are all unique skills that are powerful on their own but have even more impact when they are woven together as a thought process. We need to provide plenty of time for children to practise these skills in response to the questions we ask and the situations that we present to them.

Springboard ideas

Often the first idea is not the best one; but you need that first idea to springboard children's thinking on to others. It is important that children become familiar with the process of coming up with a number of ideas and not just one. To be able to do this they need to feel confident that, if an adult asks them to think again, that doesn't mean that their first thought wasn't very good. It is just that the more ideas there are to work with the better.

This is effectively translated to children when adults model it by verbalising their own thinking process, for example: 'That was a great idea I had; but I wonder if I can think of another one?'

There are some things that can get in the way of talk for thinking:

* **Adult-dominated conversations** – studies of interaction in education settings over the last fifty years have consistently shown that it is teacher-talk that dominates the classroom and that in much of this talk there is a lack of open questioning. Such studies show that, often in adult-led discussions, closed questions predominate. Children only make brief responses; adult-talk rarely challenged children's thinking, and child-to-child discussions were rare.

* **Closed questions** – an open question is one that allows for a range of possible answers. A closed question allows for only a true or false answer. One of the problems that results from adults using too many closed questions is that it leads to a decline in children's curiosity.

* **Telling not teaching** – allowing children to reach a correct conclusion under their own steam can be a long and arduous process. Sometimes they need to repeat the same activity several times and get the same result before they can work out what they need to do differently to move their thinking forward. There are occasions when it would be much quicker and simpler just to 'tell' the child the right answer. However, unless they have gone through the evaluation process themselves, then the 'telling' is likely to have little impact on their learning.

There are some things that you can do to help the children by creating opportunities for talk development:

I think that...

* **Enquiry talk** – through asking questions and posing problems with questions such as: What do you want to find out? Why do you think that happened? How do you think …? When might you need to use that?

* **Reasoning talk** – encouraging children to talk about why they think something should happen, or why they think they should have what they want when they want it. In simple terms, can they give a reason for why things happen and also on a more personal level why they have particular preferences?

* **Creative thinking talk** – getting children to apply imagination to their thinking to look for alternative explanations and ideas. Ask questions such as: How could you have done that differently? What if there wasn't a ….? How would it work if you couldn't use the …?

* **Evaluation talk** – it is an important part of the children's learning process for them to be able to have time to reflect on what they have learned. We can prompt this process by asking them open questions and giving them time to consider their response. The classic parent question of 'What did you do at school today?' will usually result in the response, 'Nothing!' That is because the question is too broad and there is usually insufficient time given for an appropriate response.

Often, to produce a good thought takes time. Young children sometimes need lots of time to make sense of what they have experienced, match it to what they already know and then use that information to come up with a new thought. In my work with the following setting (see over) we turned what could have been a gerbil disaster into an opportunity for the children to use their knowledge to come up with a gerbil solution!

A day in the life of ABC

We will get there with the new boy — it will just take a bit longer! He has very limited speech and assumes that every time you speak directly to him you are telling him off and cries (loudly)! He cannot sit or stay still for any length of time, so if we do gather at any point he cries (loudly)!

The talk area is looking lovely — we finished the wallpapering yesterday. In an effort to make it feel even more like a little bit of home I have decided to put a television in it. But being the talk space it can't be any normal TV; this needs to be a TV to talk about.

Our site manager got me an old television and very kindly stripped the insides out. I just left it in the middle of the carpet for the children to discover. As I had anticipated, it caused a lot of good talk!

The following TV idea I have to thank my father for. When my brother and I were little we got some gerbils from school (the school gerbil gave birth unexpectedly)! We didn't have a cage so my dad took the insides out of an old TV set and filled it with sawdust so that we could watch the gerbils on TV! The memory of how ace it was has always stuck with me.

Friday was a good day although the children are clearly shattered by the end of the week. We have had a new starter this week and he is very immature and needy and is having a huge impact on the environment and how it is running.

So, guess what is coming to my TV? Yep, gerbils! I have spent most of the day blocking up holes in the set and also cutting some perspex and sticking it to the front for a screen. I also got carried away and cut a hole in the top and mounted an aquarium spotlight (which is no mean feat for a man who has to 'get somebody in' to change a plug). The silicone is drying as we speak.

Two weeks later

The gerbils have been with us for two weeks now and they are a GREAT success. The children absolutely love them. They are on a table in our talk area (opposite the sofa) and we 'switch on' the gerbil TV by turning on the light. They are fascinating to watch and talk about.

All was going well until we discovered yesterday that 'someone' has cracked the Perspex screen and all three gerbils had escaped. The Headteacher took the decision to close for the day whilst the escapees were captured. All of the Nursery staff were on 'gerbil watch'! Unfortunately, despite the closure and the complete emptying of the stock cupboard. No gerbils were recovered!

Three weeks later

I walked in today, switched on the light and there were two gerbils in the middle of the carpet — just looking at me. They let me walk right up to them, bend over and then VAMOOSH! They were off! I then sat in the talk area for twenty minutes while both of the escapee gerbils scurried around me, even sniffing my hand. But as soon as I moved as much as an eyebrow ... they were gone!

In the end I constructed a tunnel of cardboard boxes along the skirting board and herded them into a corner where I could get them! So after half an hour of hoofing around they were both back in the telly!

When I told the children they were full of it, so I decided to go with my first instinct and offer them the opportunity to design a 'gerbil catcher'! The boys were really keen and most of them ended up working together to make a collaborative design. There was LOTS of discussion about what they were going to have and how it was going to work. They ended up spending a long time working on it and produced a really detailed drawing which they were all very proud of.

The girls enjoyed talking about it; but fewer of them actually went on to produce anything. As often happens, one child produced something WAY beyond my expectation of her ability. She worked alone at the workshop for quite a while.

And then produced this ...

So much thought had gone into every aspect of it. For a child who does not usually produce a great deal it was a huge self-esteem boost.

One girl drew a picture that was quite random and so I did the usual: 'That looks like a brilliant gerbil catcher; tell me all about it.' After a suitable pause and a look of disdain she said, 'It's a cat' and walked off. They never fail to make you chuckle!

Chapter 5

Talk for reflecting

The ability to be able to reflect on what you have done and then make changes as a result is a complex skill. Children have to be aware that their actions and words can have an impact on others and their environment before they can begin to consider how they might say or do things differently. Children need to be coached through this idea of cause and effect and adults need to model and support the type of talk that will help children to hone their skills.

Understanding the process of reflection

Reflection is not always a formal thought-out process. Natural reflection may well come when we think about something that we have already done that went well and made us feel good, or something that did not go so well and made us feel bad. When children are in the early stages of this development, it can be hard for them to be able to express what they are feeling because they don't have the words to be able to talk about how they feel.

Reflection can also be a more structured way of getting children to think and talk in order to deal with a problem. This type of reflection may take place when we give children time to stand back from something, or talk it through, a tactic often used when dealing with examples of unacceptable behaviour. Talk for reflection helps children to develop a problem-solving approach.

There are some things that can get in the way of encouraging reflective talk:

• **Too little time** – In order to reflect, children need to be given time between the event and the reflection. They also need to be given an appropriate amount of time to carry out their reflection. This can take quite a while depending on the child.

• **Not enough vocabulary** – even if they are able to reflect at some level about what they have done, some children will find it hard to articulate their feelings because they don't have an appropriate level of vocabulary. This will come through effective modelling from adults and lots and lots of opportunities to practise.

• **Lack of strategies** – as talking in a reflective manner is not familiar or automatic to the majority of children, they need to be given prompts and strategies to help them refine the skill.

There are some things that you can do to help children by creating opportunities for reflection:

◆ **Make sense of experiences** – plan to talk with the children to help them make sense of the experiences that they have, both the mundane and the spectacular. Make sure that you have provision in place that gives them the freedom to role-play and revisit the things that are going on in their lives. Making sense of an experience will help children to learn from it.

◆ **Take time** – it can be hard to reflect when we are caught up in an activity. Make time to talk about what is happening or has just happened.

◆ **Repeat, repeat, repeat** – you may well need to revisit opportunities to talk again about an event that has occurred. Children will often remember different details and talk differently about a situation when they revisit it for the second or third time.

◆ **Bring the language of 'balance'** – one of the more advanced aspects of reflective talk is having the ability and the vocabulary to see a situation from someone else's point of view. This can be incredibly difficult for lots of children (and adults), so it is important that we remind them that others will have thoughts and feelings too that might not be the same.

◆ **Cut to the chase!** – while it is really important that you take time to listen to and support children through their reflective talk, the main point can often go astray as the children's thought and talk processes wander! It is useful to sum up what is being said by asking the child if your interpretation of it is correct and, at the same time, model language structures and vocabulary.

◆ **Check their understanding** – you can be taught the mechanisms of reflective talk, but only meaningful understanding and genuine insight will demonstrate the children's ability to truly reflect. By sensitive questioning and careful listening an adult can judge children's depth of understanding.

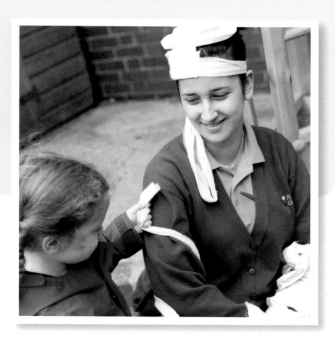

Reflecting can be a hard thing for adults to do and is not a concept that comes naturally to lots of children. Children need to be able to reflect on all aspects of their life (not just their behaviour). I had had some success using open questioning and puppets but getting children to create themselves in miniature using their own image had a significant impact on their willingness and ability to engage in reflective talk. What follows is an example of that practice in action.

A day in the life of **ABC**

Today I was working with a mixed group of Nursery and Reception children. We were looking at the concept of how children see themselves and also how to manage and enhance their interactions with others. I have done lots of sessions in the past where I have used a puppet or an imaginary friend who will display the appropriate (or inappropriate) emotion or reaction, but today I wanted to make it 'personal' to the children so we started the session by creating our very own mini-me.

What you end up with is your class in miniature. The children can then have free access to their own figures and the figures of their friends to use in the play.

Because the children have a small version of themselves, they can put themselves into role-play and small-world play like they never could before. This opens up a whole new realm of talk and language opportunities.

When I say we, the children actually had very little to do with the actual creation of their mini-me; that was handled by a 'crack team' of staff who worked a laminator like I have never seen a laminator worked before!

The idea behind a mini-me is that the children create a miniature of themselves that they can then use in their play.

First you take a full length photograph of each child, so that they fill the picture head to toe. Then you print it out, cut around the outline, laminate it and stick it to a small plastic bottle (the sort that probiotic drinks come in).

Where the staff had already identified personal or social issues with individual or groups of children, they were able to re-create scenarios that children could visit through their mini-me figures, only this time find a better solution and then talk about why it was better.

It was a very powerful and productive day — thanks to a red-hot laminator and someone who now must have a VERY healthy gut!

One of the most powerful uses for the mini-me is to get children to use theirs to reflect or discuss inappropriate behaviour and conflicts, as well as situations they have found difficult and ones they have enjoyed.

What we found was that, because the children were speaking through a mini-me, they were able to be far more honest and open about what they were thinking and feeling. The children were happier to talk about themselves because they didn't see the 'miniatures' as the same as them!

Chapter 6

Talk for imitating

> The little child, up to the age of seven, up to the change of teeth, is essentially imitative. He learns by doing what he sees being done around him. Fundamentally, all activities of the child's early years are imitations.
>
> **Steiner**

This is no different for talk. Children will copy not only the words that we use but also the speech patterns and expressions that we use while we are speaking. The more language children are exposed to, then, the more they have to draw on for their own talk. Children's language skills are not static; they grow as the children are exposed to both new talk experiences and opportunities to practise and consolidate ones that they have already had. The ability of children to develop their language and talk is directly proportionate to the quality of the talk and language that is being used in the environment around them. Limited input will result in limited output.

Accumulating vocabulary

> In four years ... an average child in a professional family would have accumulated experience with almost 45 million words, an average child in a working class family would have accumulated experience with 26 million words, and an average child in a welfare family would have accumulated experience with 13 million words.
>
> **(Hart and Risley, 2003)**

Children need to have a good mix of contextualized talk, which is often simple, short, to the point, factual and about 'now'. They also need planned experiences for de-contextualized talk, which is far more descriptive and can relate to real or imaginary situations. It is used through the telling of a fictional story or the recounting of a prior event.

Some things can get in the way of talk for imitating. These include:

◆ **Limited interactions** – from birth children need to be talked to and with in a variety of contexts with a variety of other adults and children. Children can only imitate what they can see and hear, so adults need to play an active role in initiating and developing talk.

◆ **No time to practise** – sometimes adults are so keen to engage in talk with children that they do not give them any opportunity to respond or enough time to imitate and practise what they have just heard. There is a fine balance between not talking enough and talking too much. Adults need to make quality time and provision for children to rehearse the use of new language.

◆ **Scared to get it wrong** – we often find ourselves laughing at what children say and the way that they say it. While it is important to have an element of shared humor between adults and children, the key is that the humor should be shared and not at the expense of the children's errors.

These are are some things that you can do to help children develop talk for imitating:

✳ **Model** – by demonstrating to the children that you are going to use a word or phrase that you heard someone else use. Make it obvious.

✳ **Use humour** – especially if you want children to imitate the use of grammar. Phrases like 'Can I 'av toilet' can be corrected by just repeating the correct use of language, but are much more likely to have impact and lodge themselves in the children's memory if done with a bit of humour.

✳ **Have a cunning plan** – by targeting individual or groups of children for a specific type of talk development through imitation. That way you can ensure that what you choose to talk about is relevant and interesting to them. Your environment should be filled with lots of opportunities for talk – many will be spontaneous, but lots should also be planned.

✳ **Take the talk to them** – rather than pulling children away from an area of high engagement to 'talk' with you, take your talk focus into their play.

✳ **Fiction versus fact** – although the ability to recount a factual event accurately is an important skill, telling stories is far more effective in developing children's use of a wide range of vocabulary and mechanisms of speech. The more of a 'flourish' your story has the broader the range of language that is likely to be used.

✳ **Get your grammar right** – children need to develop the knowledge that there is a way that they might talk in the playground where they can be understood by their friends and where there might be words and phrases that are only used in their part of the world. There is also a way of talking to be understood clearly by everyone anywhere who speaks the same language. If adults are going to help children to get their grammar right, then they need to be grammatically correct when they speak to them.

Experiences that really engage children will prompt the need for the use of lots of language for description as well and naming objects and emotions. If the activity involves a number of processes it allows you to use the same language repeatedly which gives the children more opportunity to assimilate it in context and then repeat it in their own talk. Who would have thought that a red cabbage could hold the key to some effective language development?

A day in the life of ABC

We are doing lots of work on trying to get the children to recognize every day fruit and vegetables. We are also singing that well-known harvest song, 'Cauliflowers Fluffy' which does indeed mention many and various varieties. Today's activity came from a discussion with a child around a line in the song that says ... and cabbages green. I remarked that not all cabbages were green and the children refused to believe me. So today I took in four red cabbages (even more confusing because they are purple!) to see what they would think.

I can't look at a red cabbage without thinking of Victoria Wood!

I asked the children what they thought we could do with one of these. Again I was surprised at how long it took someone to suggest we might eat it. I talked to the children about how vegetables were sometimes used to change the colour of things and told them that we were going to use our cabbages to dye a pair of curtains for our workshop.

Once again the children all looked at me like I was mad! I told them I was going to be chopping up the cabbages and needed helpers. I also said I would love to see some artwork based on our cabbages if they fancied it. What I was chuffed about was that some of the children could tell me which two colours to mix to get purple and (from the afternoon children) how to make it lighter and darker.

They were really beautiful and a very vivid purple. We passed them around and felt them and sniffed them and then I asked the children what they thought they were — no one thought they were cabbages. The most popular suggestion? Dinosaur eggs!

Before I told them what they were I cut one in half. The knife made a really loud crunch and then squeaked as I pulled it out. This just added to the fact that there might be a dinosaur in there. I was almost sad that there wasn't.

So far we have had a raft of interesting things to paint — chickens, tortoises, gerbils, to name but a few, and the interest has always been minimal. Give them a purple cabbage and they go 'still-life crazy'. We got LOADS of artwork!

So we chopped (and, yes, that is a real knife!). No one amputated anything and they made a really good job of it.

Not nice to look at or smell! But ...

DELICIOUS! NOT.

We filled the pan and added just plain water.

Then we set it to boil and boil and boil and stink and stink and stink! Even Year 6 upstairs were complaining by the end of the day!

At the end of the session we strained the cabbage. We were all impressed by how purple the water was. I thought the children would be disgusted by the grey mush that now lay in the bottom of the pan. Far from it. They asked if they could eat some and once they started there was no stopping them. They LOVED it!

Tomorrow we are trying some samples of calico in the juice to see if they will dye. Apparently it dyes blue. ALSO if you use beetroot to dye fabric — it goes yellow!

I also found out that if you wrap an egg in a red cabbage leaf and boil it the shell turns blue. Now that sounds like something I have to try!

Chapter 7

Talk for listening

I know it sounds a bit strange but listening to others talk is the way that we learn to talk best. Listening is essential for children's early development and for some it really isn't an easy skill to master at the beginning. The ability to listen and concentrate is something that children will need to acquire over time and through practice. Once learned, the skill of listening will be used over and over to help them to understand and apply new learning.

Hearing and listening

There is a big difference between the passive skill of hearing and the active skill of listening. You can hear something and comprehend the 'noise' but make no effort to understand the source, meaning or content of that noise. When we are listening we are trying to make sense of what we hear. We match familiar sounds, words and context to what we know and try and make sense of it. How many times has someone said something to you and you have heard them but have no idea what they have said? That is because you were hearing, but not listening.

Helping children learn listening skills

Young children have far more interesting and exciting things to do than listen to you and me. Often their concentration spans are short and, even though they may start with the best of intentions, they soon tune out! Listening skills are developed, and the more children practise, the more skilled they become. The best way to get children to practise their listening skills is to give them something that they want to listen to. I appreciate that this is not 'rocket science', but you would be amazed at how many practitioners are surprised when their children tune out during very dull or inappropriate talk input.

Reading to children and storytelling from memory is a great way to get children listening for a prolonged period of time – providing that your story is interesting!

There are lots of things that will get in the way of children's listening development. These include:

- **Being bored** – some children struggle to listen for long periods of time so build up gradually. Also, make sure that what they are listening to is interesting or relevant. The less interesting it is the quicker they will stop listening.

- **Distraction** – there are lots of distractions in our everyday life, both at home and in our settings. Young children are easily distracted (especially if they are bored). Try and make sure that when you are delivering planned talk sessions distractions are kept to a minimum, especially things like background noise, television, computers, interactive whiteboards and loud adults!

- **Crowds** – some children find it really hard to concentrate in large groups of children where there are lots of distractions and, also, lots of children en masse can make some children very nervous. Listening is often best done in small groups with a focus, rather than in larger group discussions where everyone has to share something boring like what they did at the weekend!

These are some things that you can do to help with talk for listening:

- **Establish expectations** – be clear about what 'good listening' looks like. How can the children show you through their body language and eye contact that they are listening to you? (You still can't guarantee that they are listening, but at least it is a head start). Have they stopped what they were doing? Are they looking at you? Do they acknowledge that you spoke to them? If you need them to, can they tell you what you said?

- **Keep it short** – especially with children who are just beginning to learn to listen. 'Little and often' is a good mantra to remember.

- **Get their attention!** – let the children know that it is time for them to listen. For children who are developing listening skills, remind them of what listening looks like. Use simple engaging tactics like saying a child's name before you start to speak to them.

- **Be a good role model** – children learn so much by example. It is important that adults demonstrate good listening skills, both when listening to each other and when listening to children.

Listening is such an obvious and key skill for children's development. It is not creating opportunities that promote listening that is the issue. The key is to create opportunities that make children want to listen. If you can link those opportunities to learning then all the better. In the following activity I wanted to link children's interests to listening and language skills through coverage of knowledge and understanding of the world. Well you can't knock a boy for trying!

A day in the life of ABC

I've been wanting to enhance my sand tray for a while. The children have now added so much water to it (on the sly) that it would take at least a month to dry out!

My teaching assistant dumped a bag of compost in the tray yesterday and today we added some signs of autumn for the children to discover. We have looked at the trees in the playground, discussed the leaves changing colour and had the odd random conker brought in; but I really wanted to have the opportunity to focus in on the language in a small-group situation, so we buried them in the compost (that is, we buried said signs of autumn, not the small group ...).

I had just the BEST time working with the children digging for the autumn treasures. Their enthusiasm was infectious and at some point all of the adults spent some time digging. That was until we discovered that there were live things in the tray. When we tipped it out yesterday there were a fair few slugs. Today ... not a slug to be found! Plenty of other mini-beasts though!

You can see the concentration!

This little chap caused MASS HYSTERIA and that was just from the staff!

I get the feeling that this will run and run. Have GOT to utilize it for other things as the level of engagement was so high.

If that wasn't excitement enough, we did our dyeing today — I was really pleasantly surprised with the outcome. Even though it was only two days ago, it was like pulling teeth with some of the children just to recall what we had done with the cabbages; but we got there in the end!

I debated about using elastic bands to tie-dye the material as they are really fiddly. In the end I decided to use them to differentiate for those children we had already identified as being able to triangulate. The others worked with the adults' help. Lots of children managed it well independently.

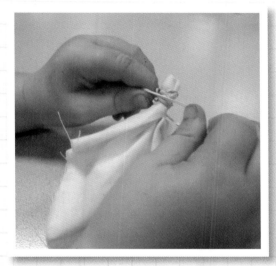

The children then dipped the fabric in the cabbage water (which really STANK), gave the pieces of material a squeeze and then we put them in the tumble-drier so that they would be dry by the end of the session.

I wasn't sure how to fix the colour, though I had read a number of articles that suggested salt and vinegar. In the end I went for salt as we had loads for our dough area. I don't know if it has worked and I don't intend to wash them to find out!

Here are the results ...

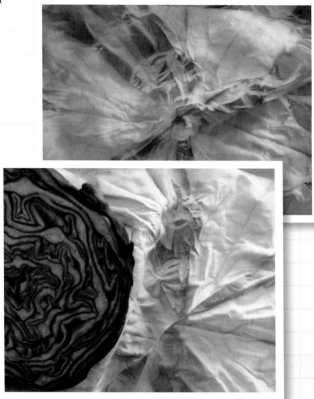

They were really blue with some more subtle shades of purple. The children were really pleased with the results.

It was only at the end of the process when I was talking to the children about this vegetable that was a cabbage but didn't look like a cabbage, that was bright purple but was called 'red', and produced purple water, when boiled, that dyed fabric blue, that I suddenly appreciated how confusing it must be to be three and discovering this weird old world for the first time!

Chapter 8

Talk for questioning

Children's use of their talk for questioning usually develops from needing to express what they want through early language development. You don't often hear toddlers ask, 'Why can't you see the moon during the day?' But they will say, 'Can I have?' The complexity of children's questioning language and talk grows as their language and experience develop.

The level of skill that children have in questioning when they come to school is directly linked to their general communication skills and the amount of purposeful interaction they have had with significant adults and their peers.

Different types of questions

There are lots of different types of questions and, therefore, a huge range of talk for questioning.

It is very easy just to think of talk for questioning as starting with who, what, where, when, how and why. These are a very good starting point and do begin the majority of question sentences that an EYFS child would use. But, for the more able talker, there are a whole range of other words that can be used to start a question like: can, would, do, could and so on. As with all teaching, you should differentiate your talk depending on the knowledge, understanding and vocabulary of the child.

Here are some things that can get in the way of talk for questioning:

◆ **Lack of interest** – if a child isn't interested in a resource or an activity, they are not likely to want to ask questions about it. Choose resources and experiences that are going to appeal to children, not just adults.

◆ **Not enough opportunities** – opportunities to ask low-level questions like 'Can I have?' will occur fairly regularly in any early years setting. We all need to be aware of the level of questioning talk of our children and then plan purposeful activities and interactions that will enhance and extend their use of talk language.

◆ **Lack of time** – for quality talk to develop, children need time to experience the talk, make sense of it and then have a go at using it.

◆ **Poor modelling** – if children never hear higher level questioning language being used then they won't have an opportunity to learn it. As adults we need to model use of this type of talk regularly so that children can become very familiar with it.

There are many things that you can do to help develop talk for questioning. One of them is to understand how questioning talk works. There is a structure to different types of questioning. I have based the following list on the work of Benjamin Bloom and Bloom's Taxonomy of the Cognitive Domain. Use all of these with the children:

* **Questioning talk for knowledge** – this is the most straightforward and simple question talk that often develops naturally in children. It is often driven by basic wants and needs (Can I have ...?) and is also demonstrated in their recall of dates, events and places, facts, basic concepts of the world and answers.

* **Questioning talk for understanding** – here children are encouraged to ask questions that will help them to articulate their understanding and meaning of what they know, for example: Does this happen because ...? Was it ...? When did...?

* **Questioning talk for applying** – this sort of questioning involves getting the children to use what they know in a new or different context, for example:. Would this happen if I did this because ...? Do you think I could use this for this because ...?

* **Questioning talk for analysis** – here children are encouraged to check that their thinking is correct. This thinking should show that they are making links between what they know and what they think might happen based on what they know. Does this happen because ...? Should I put that there because ...?

* **Questioning talk for synthesis** – synthesis just means combining old and new ideas together to make something different. Through your questioning you are going to prompt the children to try using what they know and what they think to create questions of their own about what might happen.

* **Questioning talk for evaluation** – this is the most advanced level of talk for questioning, as you are asking the children to use all of the other elements of questioning talk to explain their ideas and ask questions about why things might have happened and why things did or didn't work.

Can I have ...?

Was it ...?

If you want children to be able to practise their questioning skills, not only do adults have to model appropriate language and effective use of questioning, we also have to create opportunities and activities that will inspire children to ask questions. Prompting talk around subjects that you know children are interested in will usually do the trick nothing beats a bit of awe and wonder. Create an unusual opportunity or show them a unique resource and you are usually onto a winner. To get these children asking questions I took one of my chickens on a visit to Nursery and Reception...

A day in the life of **ABC**

Betty, one of my Orpington chickens was a big hit with staff and children alike and we got LOADS from her visit!

I set her up in the talk area in a broody cage, complete with pre-laid egg. The children have to walk past this area to hang up their coats and I was convinced one of them would see her, but no one did.

I gathered the children and asked where Betty was and who had invited her in the first place? We decided that she might be shy and hiding somewhere so we went on a Betty search until eventually she was found — with GREAT excitement!

We talked about her, looked at her, got her out and stroked her. We identified her body parts, talked about poo and where eggs come from, looked at her feathers in the sun and discovered some were green.

Then it was time to go and do 'stuff'. Betty had indeed caused a great deal of interest but it was OK if some children didn't want to go off and do 'Betty-inspired' work. At one time I would have set up my environment with everything themed around Betty; but experience has shown me that some children have limited interest and after experiencing the experience they want to do something different — and that is OK. Their levels of engagement and therefore attainment are likely to be significantly higher if they are doing something that they actually want to do.

The children had been fascinated by Betty's red wattle and crown and they feature a great deal in the work they went on to produce. We also had a lot of discussion about the green shimmer in her feathers and, again, lots of children went on to mix green paint in with the black when painting Betty's portrait.

When our lovely head came down, the children were really eager to share their new-found chicken knowledge!

We scrambled the egg in the diner ...

... and all vowed never to eat chicken again! It was a great day and I loved it!

Also, I got the children to fill the water tray both in the morning and the afternoon — so that is another job crossed off our list!

Very soon we will be redundant!

Can't wait for tomorrow to see what will develop from the Betty Factor!

Chapter 9

Talk for cooperation

There is a difference between cooperative and collaborative talk with children. When we are encouraging individual children to use their talk to contribute to an activity or discussion, it is very much just to give us their own personal thoughts. This type of talk is often used to rehearse and promote the language and behaviour that children associate with cooperation.

We develop children's ability to listen to others for extended periods of time, to wait for their turn to speak, not to interrupt, and to maintain eye contact with the speaker. It is through cooperative talk activities that we allow children to observe and rehearse the language and behaviours that we equate with being a 'good' listener and 'appropriate' talker.

It is conforming to these social norms that young children find very difficult. On the whole they are very ego-driven because, at their stage of development, most lack empathy with others. Therefore, when there is a thought in their head, it has to come straight out of their mouths – they don't see why they should wait until you or anyone else has finished what you were saying. It wasn't that interesting anyway!

Some things that get in the way of cooperative talk:

◆ **Lack of language** – when children do not have or understand the language they need for cooperative talk then they tend to be very isolated in their play and limited in their interactions. This lack of talk can often result in children using a physical response rather than a verbal one.

◆ **Not enough practice** – like with many other elements of talk, the children's ability to demonstrate it successfully is not exclusively tied to their age but more their stage of development. The one thing that helps children to develop talk above everything else is effective modelling from another child or adult and LOTS of opportunities to practise. Children do not recognize the need to practise themselves, so it is our role to provide an environment that actively promotes practice where we have identified a need.

◆ **Unequal opportunities** – cooperative talk is often dominated by one voice; often this will be the adult who is leading the activity or session, or the child who has the most well-developed talk strategies. If a cooperative talk activity has been specifically planned then we need to ensure that the children who will benefit from it most have an opportunity to participate.

Here are some things you can do to help develop talk for cooperation:

* **Assess before you start** – be clear about what sort of talk you are trying to develop in any of the activities that you plan. Clearly identify the children that need more experience of cooperative talk and ensure that they have maximum opportunity to take part.

* **Keep it interesting** – if you are trying to get children to engage in cooperative talk then you need to ensure that they are interested enough to want to engage. If the topic of conversation is dull or irrelevant then the children will either disrupt or disengage.

* **Provoke** – the aim of this type of talk activity is to get children to experience a situation where cooperation is needed, experience and effective model of cooperative talk and use for cooperative language, rehearse their version of what they have seen and then apply what they know. When these situations arise naturally within play, you are not always in a position to understand what has taken place, formulate an effective response, model that response and then create opportunities for consolidation. You may well be sorting out who hit whom first! So, if you identify a need for this type of talk development, create 'planned' scenarios within the context of play (as opposed to always sitting in a circle on the carpet) to implement and practise.

* **Promote** – actively promote, both visually and verbally, examples of appropriate use of cooperative talk, especially in response to those children who need to practise the most.

The more children there are in any one space then the more they are going to have to cooperate with each other to get what they want and to keep their play running smoothly. By restricting numbers of children in specific areas we are also restricting the potential for them to learn to be successful cooperates. So as long as it is safe, why restrict the numbers?

A day in the life of ABC

Today was a bit of a blur! We had three new starters (one whirlwind, one refuser and one screamer), a vomit incident (into the dough), a water-tray leak, followed by what happens when you leave two boys in the sand while you are distracted by a whirlwind, a refuser, a vomiter and a screamer...

Yes, that would be every sand-play toy we possess plus half a gallon of water – so much for teaching them to fill the water tray by themselves! I have to say, though, they had a GREAT time and I did find myself having a sneaky splash!

Oh, and I also had to meet with the Governing Body to talk to them about what I was doing and what structures I was putting into place for long-term impact. All in all, quite a full day!

I am really pleased with how much mark making is going on at the moment, especially with the boys, who are producing LOTS. We are all using our assessment books to note down what they are doing, so that we can challenge them next time they are there. We have one child who is showing an obsession for drawing different doors. Everything he draws and paints is a door with something exciting behind it, and it is catching. We had a whole table full of children all drawing doors today.

What really excites me about the boy and his doors is that I NEVER would have had that as a theme at this stage of the year for this age children (if at all) and now, because of how our curriculum is structured, one child has inspired the others in a big way to work with doors. I will now run with this and layer my knowledge of where the children need to go (informed by assessment) on top!

If we had been doing the topic 'Ourselves' then there would not have been space to run with an interest in spiders.

We had a special visitor...

I know – it was HUGE. It was found on the coat of a hysterical Reception child who went for help only to find two hysterical Reception staff. It took one of my fearless TA's to come to the rescue and release it. After we had all had a good look, of course!

There is such a wealth of opportunity for engaging children out there every single day. You just have to be on the look-out for it.

The other thing I have done today is to get rid of the 'Only three children can play here' signs that were dotted about.

I have never regulated the number of children in an area, as I think with proper modelling it is not an issue. Very occasionally, if I feel it is unsafe, I might ask the children to think again, but I have honestly found that they do it themselves.

If you find that all of your children want to be in one place, you have to ask yourself what is good about that place and what isn't about everywhere else. Then do something about it!

Today was also the birthday of my little friend who said, on her first day, that she hadn't heard what I said because she couldn't be bothered listening to me! Over the weeks I have grown to absolutely love her — she really makes me laugh.

We sang happy birthday to her — I played my Beano guitar. None of the children sang (bar one, who just shouted the last word of every line). It was like something out of an institution!

I then asked her if she would like to pick a song to sing as it was her special day ... She would and she would like ...

'Serumphlin Cub'

'Sorry? Say that again for me — I am a bit deaf.'

'Serumphlin Cub!'

'And again?'

'I said ... Serumphin CLUB'

'Ah,' say I. 'S Club 7? Reach for the stars? Ooh, sorry I can't play that one!'

'NO!' she says, while her hands move up to her hips. 'I SAID Serumphlin Club.'

'Who sings it?' I ask.

Now, she tuts and turns her back on me with her arms folded — in a proper huff. This is a shame because I am trying hard.

'I am sorry,' I say. 'I am getting old. It's my fault ... I can't hear very well.'

She then speaks to me loudly and slowly, like I am simple: 'I want ... SEX IN THE CLUB — I dunno who says it!'

I really wasn't expecting that. All I could think to say was, 'How about Five Little Speckled Frogs?' To which she replied, 'Naaah, forgerit' and sat down.

It's Usher, by the way, who 'says it'. Sex in the Club — the choice of every four-year-old on their birthday!

Chapter 10

Talk for collaborating

When children are engaged in cooperative talk it is often about sharing their individual ideas in a shared space; whereas collaborative talk is about children using other children's or adults' ideas to add to and enhance their own and, therefore, take their learning forward. Good collaborative talk will promote simultaneous discovery amongst the group who are talking and learning together. Ideally we want all of the children to have the experience of using the talk of others to clarify their own thoughts and to use what they know to contribute to the discussion and take the others' learning forward. Children are using the experience for both clarification and input.

> 'What a child can do today with help, tomorrow he will be able to do alone.'
>
> **Vygotsky**

Creating opportunities

When we create opportunities for young children to engage in collaborative talk they have to have already shown some level of success in cooperative talking; otherwise they will not be able to collaborate and will often revert back to non-engagement or non-compliance. For collaborative talk to be successful, the children need to be able to, and have the opportunity to, share their ideas, expand their thoughts (in the early stages of collaborative talk this needs to be supported and modelled by careful adult intervention), have their thoughts challenged by others and sometimes change what they first thought as a result.

When you are grouping children for collaborative talk it helps to have children who have a similar basic level of understanding but different experiences. If you have a very broad mix of children, then the children who have a more limited level of understanding will be unable to take part in the talk and will revert to either inappropriate contributions or no contribution at all.

Some things that can get in the way include:

- **Teaching too much too soon** – We often try and encourage young children to engage in collaborative talk long before they have the skills to do so and then wonder why it doesn't work! Large circles of children on the carpet are not conducive to its development. Smaller groups of children who are at similar stages in their development will produce much better attainment levels.

- **Boredom** – Collaborative talk is all about sharing your thoughts and opinions. When children are really keen to share with you, then create multiple opportunities to reinforce good talk skills and model practice. Spontaneous talk will always crop up around an area of interest (that is why the children are talking about it!). If you are planning a talk activity make sure it is something that will actually get them talking, not fiddling with their Velcro!

- **Criticism** – If a child is heading in the wrong direction or is articulating inaccurate knowledge they need to be steered sensitively in the right direction. This is best done through further questioning and explaining, rather than just telling them they are wrong. Poor self-esteem is one of the greatest inhibitors to success, especially in boys; so gently correct them by letting them think it was their idea in the first place!

- **Telling rather than guiding** – If you just tell children the answer, or give them the solution, then they will have learned nothing. The best scenario is that you guide them to the answers by giving them time to talk about what has happened and consider why, then try again. It sometimes takes considerably longer than just telling, but the learning is so much better.

Some things that you can do to help develop talk for collaborating include:

- **Use talking partners** – Well-selected talking partners, talking trios and talk groups can have a great impact. Pairing a low attainer and a high attainer together in the hope that the low attainer will glean 'pearls of wisdom' from the high attainer has limited success. Both children need to share a common level of ability to understand a concept even if their experiences of it have been different.

- **Develop having opinions** – Encourage children to have an opinion and give them opportunities to express it to others. Get into the habit of asking them to explain why they feel the way they do. If they cannot articulate the reason then you can clearly see where they need support in their 'talk for learning' development.

- **Ask questions** – The best way to extend children's talk and thinking is by asking them a question – ideally not just any random question off the top of your head, but one that will challenge them to think again about something or extend their response. It is also a good idea to encourage children to question each other about what they are saying and doing and anything that they don't understand. Initially this process can be a bit painful and the questions very closed and often unrelated to the subject – but persevere, and good modelling and lots of practice can make even very young children into effective questioners.

- **Be a good listener** – Not only are you modelling one of the key skills for collaborative talk but you are also showing children that you value what they are saying enough to stop and listen.

- **Repeat** – Often, when young children are talking, they will use fifty words where one would have done. That use of extra language also serves to side-track them on to other thoughts and subjects that were not related to the one they started. Repeating back the key points to children shows them that you were listening and encourages them to order their thinking.

- **Don't accept the first answer** – By the same token don't dismiss it, but try and use further open questioning to facilitate a broader explanation or further investigation. (Word of warning: don't always follow every answer with another question. Answering questions can be hard work and, if someone keeps asking you a question that makes your head hurt, then you will stop volunteering answers!)

Shared interest or shared desire is what brings children together in a play situation. Knowing what engages your children and then ensuring that your environment supports their collaboration in exploring that interest will go a long way to ensuring that they get lots of opportunities to work and play collaboratively. In this setting, the children had shown an interest and enjoyment in building but building can be a solo activity if you just take your own small pile of bricks. So, we made the building materials so big that not only did they create maximum engagement, the children had to cooperate to achieve their goal – the tallest tower in the world!

A day in the life of ABC

Is a tower ever too tall?

I have always been bemused by the signs that I see in settings that say construction can only be built to shoulder height. Why? So many opportunities are being missed if we put restrictions like that on children.

If you are really going to learn some fundamental laws of physics, it is difficult to do so with ten small blocks! You need to have the thrill of your tower wobbling and then not falling over and the sheer joy of a monumental tumble!

So, how high is too high? Well, that is really based on what you feel comfortable with. Although if you only allow building to shoulder height, I would encourage you to try and extend your comfort zone a little bit.

Apart from having the BEST time building with the children today, the fact that I let them go as high as they dared allowed me to observe a child use all of his problem-solving know-how to figure out how we could make the tower taller once he could no longer reach. Through this process he demonstrated that he had some quite sophisticated problem-solving strategies.

As I have said in my previous posts the construction at the school that I am consulting in is severely lacking and doesn't allow for much differentiation or progression.

I am in the process of remedying that but, in the meantime, one of our parents donated a load of flat-pack boxes that were perfect for a bit of large-scale work.

When we were making up the boxes one boy decided that we needed to write what was in them on the outside. He managed about ten before the novelty wore off, but I was impressed that he had been inspired to write in the first place.

Clearly higher than shoulder height and achieved after many failed attempts. Mr Clegg helped with the top ones!

The other good thing about this activity was that the children had to talk to each other. Initially they all just wanted to put the next box on top. They soon realized that if two or more people went at the same time the whole thing fell down. Someone had to take charge! Again, I was surprised at who that was. It wasn't the 'usual' leaders but our boy who is fixated by doors. I was impressed at his boldness and persuasiveness, but not by what he managed to build!

What do you do when you can't reach and Mr Clegg is busy? Some of us stand and stare; some suggest throwing a box up (with disastrous consequences). One boy begins to quietly collect and stack chairs!

I had no intention of letting him stand on stacked chairs and in the setting there aren't enough chairs anyway, but I wanted to be able to praise his ingenuity and I wanted him to realize that a stack of chairs were not right for the job.

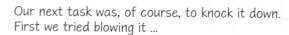

Our next task was, of course, to knock it down. First we tried blowing it ...

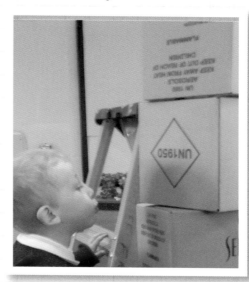

When someone comes up with the suggestion to get a ladder ... you raid the caretaker's cupboard!

Then you get building. Climbing as high as you feel comfortable and feeling the fear when you have taken a step too high. As an adult observing I would obviously not let a child take a risk that I felt was dangerous, but climbing up one step at a time was within the boundaries of health and safety!

But no joy there — even when we all joined in. So it came down to the 'good old shove' to do the job. It was supposed to be on the count of three; but someone just couldn't contain themselves and shoved after two! The culprit has to date gone undiscovered.

Oh, and what did our door-fixated boy make with the boxes?

A door of course!

You can see why they might get butterflies in their tummy. It must feel very high up.

But just look what you can build! I cannot tell you the excitement this structure caused or how pleased the children were who had helped to build it.

We got SO much out of a pile of cardboard boxes and the engagement levels were so high. I think it is an activity that will run and run. It was also very purposeful and calming for our more boisterous boys who really enjoyed being focused.

Chapter 11

Talk for sharing

(conflict resolution)

Talking to resolve conflict is a necessity for all early years settings. Often, the younger the children are the harder they find it to articulate what they want to say or see the reason WHY they have to compromise or share.

Lots of practitioners will say that first children or only children are the worst at sharing; but research has shown that it is actually the second or third (and any subsequent children) that have the greatest issues with sharing. Just because they are required to do it at home does not seem to make them 'better' at it. If anything they fight harder to keep something for themselves!

How children handle conflict

Different children handle conflict in different ways; this is often regardless of their language ability. Boys tend to be more physical in their attempts to find a resolution to the issue and girls tend to be more verbal.

Children's views of the right and wrong way to resolve a conflict can be greatly distorted by their home model. It is imperative that we have a good understanding of how our children view effective conflict resolution before we start to impose our systems. A child's emotional competence plays a part in their ability to understand how their actions will affect the feelings of others. One of the most effective ways to help children to develop their emotional competence is through allowing them to engage in greater levels of pretend play.

Through an understanding of how and why children react in the way that they do to conflict, we can plan specific talk activities that will enable them to rehearse appropriate responses and begin to empathize with the feelings of others.

Things that can get in the way of talk for conflict resolution include:

◆ **Adult intervention** – Sometimes as an adult we can just step in and resolve the conflict by closing down play or removing the item that has caused the upset. This just teaches the children that they do not need to reach an agreeable conclusion; the most powerful member of the group is able to make the ultimate decisions.

◆ **Lack of language** – When children are unsure of what to say or lack the vocabulary to be able to say it they will often resort to a more physical resolution.

◆ **Asking silly questions** – As part of the resolution process of a conflict we will often ask children, 'Why did you do that?' More often than not they will give the answer, 'I don't know'. That is because they genuinely don't know and, even if they did, they would probably not have the language or thought processes in place to be able to break it down into its composite parts!

◆ **Not enough time or space to practise** – To allow children to really begin to understand the thoughts and feelings of others, you have to put them into 'other children's shoes'. One of the best and 'safest' places to do this is through role-play. This sort of role-play needs to be unstructured (deconstructed) so that children have the freedom to apply their play to scenarios that are relevant to them. It might be quite difficult to work on 'outdoor conflict resolution' in the veterinary surgery role-play area.

Here are some things you can do to help talk for sharing:

* **Be a good example** – tell children they can feel any way they wish, but they must control what they do. Make sure you are not telling them to stop shouting at each other when you shout at them.

* **Encourage language for problem-solving** – with very young children, this is more about modelling the appropriate language and behaviour that you would like to see them use. With more mature children, it is introducing them to the variety of possibilities that there are for resolving conflict.

* **Be an interpreter** – be on hand to help children interpret their emotions. Lots of children don't know why they feel the way that they do and often haven't got a name for it. Take time to help them articulate their feelings and discuss possible resolutions they might try next time.

* **Offer regular play in a positive setting** – appropriate play alongside a well-informed adult gives children abundant chances to practise conflict resolution. Regularly audit your provision to check that you have lots of activities and games that encourage turn taking. Have you also got some activities that will require the children to share? Are you using these as a teaching tool?

* **Explain that there is a choice** – be really clear with children about the choices they have. When some children back themselves into a corner, they think that they have no option other than to keep going.

* **Make your expectations clear** – regardless of the child's home model, make it clear what your behavioural expectations are. Whenever aggression occurs, make it clear that that behaviour is not acceptable. Remember to always stress that it is the behaviour that you don't approve of, not the child.

* **Guide with questions** – resist separating children, isolating them on a 'naughty chair', or telling them exactly what to do. Instead, talk to them and take them through the basic steps of problem-solving. It is important that each child has a chance to speak and that the conversation is not dominated by any one child. Ask questions that encourage them to analyze what has just happened and look for solutions.

* **Accentuate the positives** – whenever you see successful conflict resolution taking place, make a fuss of it. All of your children need to get the clear message that that was the right way to do it and, as a result, positive things have happened.

* **Make it better** – after a conflict most young children are happy to go back to their play; but some need support in how they can know and show that everything has been resolved successfully. Sometimes being made by an adult to 'say sorry' and then uttering the word sorry does not mean that the children actually are. This will be felt by everyone involved. Sometimes for a rushed adult it is a 'quick fix' that allows them to get on. It is a valuable process to talk to all of your children about other ways that they can show they are sorry and then use that list when the time comes.

A day in the life of ABC

As far as I'm concerned it's perfectly acceptable to say to the boys that they can play their game but not when it destroys the work of other children because that is inappropriate.

It was suggested that we ban gun play; but I know from experience that that would be fruitless, as we would just drive it underground and they would do it anyway. So ...

I asked the team to identify the play that the boys were engaging in. I also asked them to accept that it was 'normal' play for children of this age and talked a bit about why they play that way.

I then asked the team how we could use that play to our advantage rather than fight against it. If the boys only ever run, around day after day, playing the same game in an environment as big as ours, you have to ask what is NOT going on in the other areas to tempt them.

The upshot is that we are going to turn the soon-to-be den-making area into an army boot camp where they can play out their gun play and we can intervene and use it as a teaching opportunity.

Which brings me back to my well-worn point ... If you know that they do it and will do it even if you tell them not to, then do your job and use it as an opportunity to educate — both about the reality of guns and to teach them something.

We have had a slight change of plan for our den-making area outdoors. It came up as a result of a discussion about the boys' play! Basically, any object becomes a gun and they chase. There is LOTS of imaginative play going on, but they literally run through everything — so lots of work is being (unintentionally) interrupted or destroyed.

Documenting the setting up of the boot camp

With regard to setting up a new area indoors or out, I think it is essential that you document why you are doing it and exactly what it is you hope to gain from it — especially if, like Pete, you are expecting Ofsted at any time!

These were my thoughts around how we would set up our armyboot camp.

Setting up an 'army boot camp' area outdoors

1) Why? — Identify the reason for setting it up

Outdoor observations have shown that there is an ongoing trend for very physical active play that is mainly initiated and dominated by boys which involves pretend guns, superheroes or combative play. Although not malicious, this play is disrupting and in some cases destroying other focused work that is taking place outdoors. The 'management' of this play is not only taking up valuable practitioner time but also stifling the opportunities that the play itself presents.

Of all of the types and themes of outdoor play that we have identified this half-term, this is the only one that has been consistently observed on a daily basis.

2) Specific needs identified — What exactly is it that you need to tackle?

The play that we have identified mainly consists of groups of boys who have an ongoing game in which they chase each other with the purpose of 'capture' or 'shooting'. At the moment they are using any non-specific item to represent a weapon and occasionally creating one from construction. One of the issues that we have identified is that the children are using inappropriate items in their play which result in either damage to the item or loss. This, in turn, has an impact on the overall level of provision that we can offer as resources are damaged or incomplete.

Even though practitioners remind these children regularly about how to play, they become very highly engaged in their play and 'forget'. This high level of engagement from a group of children who are often more difficult to engage needs to be channelled, not ignored.

3) What other elements of their play can you use to help?

Our observations have shown us that these children also show high levels of engagement in deconstructed outdoor role-play, especially the building of den-like structures with the community play blocks and tarpaulins.

4) What elements of the curriculum will you be supporting through this provision?

Communication and Language

We will provide lots of opportunities for mark making, drawing and planning. The level of engagement will allow us to introduce a great deal of language development and vocabulary. This will need just the right amount of practitioner intervention which we will review regularly. We will enhance the area with related books as appropriate.

Physical Development

The large-scale construction will develop children's spacial awareness as well as their sense of balance and proportion. The process will involve both gross- and fine-motor movement which will impact on the children's dexterity and impact upon their mark-making ability.

Personal, Social and Emotional Development

The children will be working together developing skills of sharing, complying and negotiating. They will have the opportunity to plan, discuss, build and amend their plans. The den play will allow children to produce spaces where they can feel secure and enclosed. The gun/superhero play will give them the opportunity to assimilate what they see around them and make some sense of it within their own personal context.

Mathematics

The children will have the opportunity to develop their understanding and use of mathematical language, especially related to size, length and weight.

Understanding the World

Through the construction process the children will be getting first-hand experience about how and why things work, including the effects of the weather on the structures they build and which materials are most appropriate. The opportunities for knowledge in this area are limitless. Again there needs to be careful and considered adult intervention which is regularly reviewed.

Art and Design

The children will be encouraged to develop their higher order thinking skills, finding solutions to problems and coming up with ideas for building their structures. They will then use those structures to support their imaginative play.

A day in the life of **ABC**

5) Any specific interventions to encourage maximum engagement from the children?

We are aware that this is a 'boy-dominated' area of our outdoor provision at the moment. As such we need to make sure that we use specific planned interventions to try and make this area more engaging to the girls. Our observations have shown us so far that the boys tend to do the 'construction' and the girls then do the 'enhancement' of the structure and often lead the play. The boys are very self-sufficient in their play and will often initiate an activity. The girls tend to engage better when there is also an adult present. It appears that, if the girls do initiate den construction and are then joined by a group of boys, then the boys dominate and take over.

Our adult intervention in the play needs to take all of the above into account and actively combat any negative aspects.

6) What will you create? — Using what you know

Our initial plan is to create a designated area that responds to the preferred play and personal interests of a significant number of our children. Rather than attempt to ban or ignore play that is causing us issues, but results in high levels of engagement, we are going to utilize it to achieve maximum learning impact.

How we will do this:

✦ We will establish a den-making area based around an 'army/combat' theme. The children will lead the content through a collaborative planning session. We will provide some commercial representations of weapons as well as work with the children on how to produce their own.

✦ We will establish rules about how this area is to be used and what is acceptable when it comes to weapon play. We will also be clear about the sanctions that we will put in place if the play becomes inappropriate.

✦ Because we have identified that the engagement of girls in this type of play can often be an issue, we will ensure that they are involved in the planning process and implement as many of their ideas as possible.

✦ To ensure specific impact on learning we will look at the current needs of the children identified by our most recent assessment and see which of these identified needs could be met through planning activities based on this area.

✦ We will continually carry out observations of how the area is working and evaluate its success at team meetings.

Then all you need is a basic resources list and you are away! If your team has a number of members it is a useful activity to do together because it helps you all to be sure that you understand what you are doing and why!

It also shows anyone who has to make judgements about you or your practice that what you do is based on need as well as interest and that you are monitoring and evaluating impact.

One week later

Meanwhile at 'Boot Camp'. Things are progressing really well. We have almost eradicated the anti-social, disruptive play in the outdoor area. Since it is now confined to one space, the children are investing far more time and energy in creating 'game play' rather than just chasing. There is negotiation and discussion as well as some arguments over who gets the best guns! My feeling on that is that children will never learn how to resolve an argument if they are not allowed to have one!

We were experiencing children hitting each other with the swords, even though we had made clear our policy on no body contact. We have talked a great deal with the children about why it is not a good idea to hit someone else and explored how it might make them feel. We have used our deconstructed role-play a great deal to help to model appropriate weapon play before it goes outside into the much bigger and freer environment.

What is important with an area like this is that you set ground rules and stick to them. No second chances: If you break the rule you are out — end of!

To combat this trend one of our staff gave the children fencing lessons, stressing that the more skill you had the less body contact there would be. It worked a treat — we will just have to see if they remember.

Chapter 12

Talk initiatives

The talk sofa

The idea for a 'talk sofa' came from watching a YouTube video on which Dr Chris Pascal was talking about how lots of early years environments were beginning to look more and more clinical and less and less familiar to the children that were coming to learn in them. As we know, there is a strong link between children's emotional well-being and attainment. If the children are happy and settled then they are ready to explore and learn. If they are anxious and upset then all of their energy and brain power is directed towards those feelings and not towards learning. Makes perfect sense!

What Dr Pascal suggested was that we started to add features to our environments that would help children make links to familiar objects that they would recognize from home. Not that you would want to turn your setting into a furniture showroom, or that you would fill it with impractical pieces of furniture; but that you would give some thought to positive links that you could make to a child's safe and secure environment.

When I was running talk activities in settings with children and staff, they always seemed to take place on the carpet in a circle. This would usually result in the adult leading the session, placing the children that they felt needed the most 'support' (read that as the ones with the least concentration) at either side of her/his feet. She/he would place them here because this allowed maximum behaviour management possibilities. The adult could start with a stern look, then a quiet word and then an 'appropriate' hand on the shoulder – just to remind them that she/he was watching … always watching!

The problem with this technique is that when it comes to talk and sharing in a circle of thirty children, no child really wants to go first or last. If a child goes first, then he or she has said his or her bit, and usually the sort of child who needs 'appropriate' reminders is not the sort who will happily sit and listen while twenty-nine other children say their bit! Nor do you want to be on the other side of the adult's feet as this means you go last and you HAVE to listen to twenty-nine other children before you get your go and that is usually twenty-eight children too many!

To counterbalance this arrangement the adult will usually put a flurry of 'well-behaved' girls right in the middle of the circle (about twelve o'clock). The problem with this is that well-behaved girls often have a lot to say for themselves and, once they get going, it is difficult to stop them. In fact, how can you stop them? Activities in a circle are often used to develop children's talk and confidence. You can't just say, 'OK, shush now, you are even beginning to bore me!' You just have to, 'Umm' and 'Yes' and occasionally, 'That's lovely and hope for the best'.

It is little wonder that the children at the teacher's feet are not responding to the behavioural management techniques and have crawled off to play with the construction (or if there is no construction available, often themselves!).

Large-group talk situations with young children can be a bit of disaster – especially if the topic is a really dull one, like 'news'. Sharing news on a Monday is one of those things that we feel we need to do – something that has been recorded in the Holy Grail of teaching; but nobody quite knows why.

My news about news in early years is that it is dull, well most of the time. You get the occasional birth announcement, hair cut (due to nits) or death of a pet. But other than that, children forget what they have done at the weekend or they genuinely haven't done anything exciting.

As a practitioner I used to live in fear of a Monday morning death story. It would usually start with something small like a hamster or gerbil; but then it would always snowball into what I can only describe as a 'dead-off', where children seemed to compete to see who had the most dead pets/dead relatives. It would be three hours later and I would be talking about the big book that we had just read and a hand would shoot up in response to a question about the story. In all innocence I would say, 'Yes? What do you think?' And the child would reply, 'And my Grandma is dead!' It is hard to think of a response to that really!

If you are going to do news, then I would get the children to tell somebody else's news. This gives them the opportunity to lie, without condoning lying! When children are making up stories, they tend to extend their sentences more, use higher level vocabulary and lots more descriptive phrases. They can be a fictitious character that they are interested in like Ben 10.

Or get them to make up news for someone else in the group, or even you! They usually relish the prospect of making their adult do weird and wonderful stuff during their made-up weekend. You will have to model the process a few times, but once they get the hang of it, you will get some great results.

`Hey, Ben 10 what did you do this weekend?'

I had found, through experience, that this worked much better in small groups rather than big carpet sessions, so I married the small-group talk work with the idea of linking the setting to home. That is when the 'talk sofa' concept was born.

In truth, the talk sofa was my second idea. My first was to combine focused talk with snack time. I had this vision of snack time as being really communal, where we all sat and ate together and engaged in some quality talk that had been planned in response to assessment. I did try it that way, on a number of occasions. The thing was it never quite worked out like I had planned it. For one thing it meant that we all had to have our snack at the same time. There is a fundamental flaw with that idea, and that is that not all children are hungry or thirsty at the same time. It also made my morning really fragmented and I was breaking children's engagement in their activities to tidy them away and come and have their snack.

Also it took ages to sort it out. There was talk during the snack times, but I couldn't really say that it was quality, or underpinned by planning. It was more along the lines of: Pardon? Not again! That's every day this week you have spilt your milk! Mrs Smith … THE MOP! …Just move round a bit and let her in … Don't put full milk cartons in the bin; the cleaner will complain again…What do you mean you haven't finished, you have had twenty minutes … SUCK! SUCK HARDER! Not what you would call quality talk.

I found free-flow snacks much better for facilitating quality talk in small groups where children dictated the subject matter with the odd prompt from a passing adult.

I wanted my sofa to feel like a bit of home, so it had to be a proper sofa. Not a child-sized one made out of a sponge door wedge and covered in primary-colour plastic. Everyone, including the adult, needed to feel comfortable, not sitting with their knees up to their chin and slowly sliding down until they ended up on the floor! You need to invest in a proper sofa: one that meets all of the fire safety health regulations, but one that you can sit on.

You need to be clear with the rest of the team and with the children about the purpose of this sofa. It is not a 'lie down if you feel a bit poorly' sofa or a 'dump stuff on it because you can't find anywhere else' sofa. It is a TALK sofa. If you value the power and potential of talk development with young children, then you need to give your sofa some credibility and status.

The first thing that you need to do is to 'dress' your sofa. When used at its simplest level you can just go there to talk with children about anything that they want to talk about. There are some children who might even struggle to do this. A 'dressed' sofa always gives you something to talk about. When you are thinking about what to put on your sofa, go for variety, unusual and unique. Have a good few cushions all in different sizes, shapes and textures. I always stuff mine with things like lavender, vanilla, cinnamon, lemon grass, curry powder – anything that will smell when you sniff it. Try and get hard ones, soft ones, rough ones, silky ones, fluffy ones …

You can add throws of different size, colour and texture. Use a mixture of colour and pattern. It is not meant to look like something out of an interiors magazine. It is supposed to give maximum potential for talk, experience and engagement.

Above is an example of a talk sofa in a setting. There is lots of texture, size and shape going on but (as gorgeous as it is) it is probably a little bit too over-coordinated (sorry Tracey and Val!) You can use your 'dressing' to help children to develop language to express a preference (I like this one …), or you can develop that further into extending their sentence (I like this one because…). The possibilities are endless.

Beyond the simple dressing of the sofa, you can then begin to hide interesting objects in, on and around it. I just tell the children that I have hidden something on the talk sofa and usually that is enough. If your objects are interesting then they will talk about them. I have used everything from a World War II wooden potato masher to a beaded African fertility doll. Both made great discoveries for the children to talk about, although none of the female staff would sit on the sofa once the fertility doll had been hidden in it!

Don't forget to use underneath the sofa as well. There is something quite exciting about putting your hand into the dark recesses of your talk sofa and having a feel about to see what you can find. When you are developing children's descriptive language, put a range of items under the sofa, get them to lie down on their stomachs, put one hand under the sofa and then face the other way so that they can't see what they are touching. You don't want them to tell you what they think the object is; you only want them to describe what they can feel. Some children find this quite hard. If that is the case then do lots of modelling!

Don't just take my word for it …

Dear Alistair

I mailed you a while ago to ask about 'sofa talk'. Subsequently I have introduced some of your ideas into my own setting and I thought that I would share the results with you. I'm currently involved with the ECaT project and, as a result of the action plan that I made from the ECaT audit, I realize that my focus had to be a room to encourage talk. Thus our 'Talk Room', was born!!! I used your ideas of the Talk Sofa and Talk Box; I also introduced book talk sessions and talk for writing sessions. There is also a weekly maths session that's held in their too (all child choice). So much goes on in this room I needed to make sure that there was structure for the adults to ensure that the work in there would continue to happen.

In the picture you can see the bookshelf; on that I put objects that the children have shown an interest in. I keep the area well stocked with mark-marking equipment too. I've made a number of 'grab and go' boxes ... a bit like your enhancement tubs; the idea being that we can be responsive to children's interests. Our setting had a visit from National Strategies. I credited you with Talk Sofa and this is what Roseanne Pugh had to say.

From: Pugh, Rosanne (National Strategies)

Sent: 17 February 2011 08:28

Subject: ECaT visit

… The influence of ECaT was evident through the enthusiasms of the staff and genuine unrelenting focus on the promotion of early language skills with careful consideration of the conditions for learning underpinning opportunities for talk. Use of open-ended questioning, musicality of number, possibilities for role-play and drama, attention to the outdoor environment were evident in the visit. Stimulating objects of interest provoked children's talk and dramatic play with one another. Careful attention to monitoring provides staff with the information needed for quick, responsive intervention. Children are progressing well, some with accelerated progress. The programme has built capacity within the staff team, their knowledge and practice is testament to the improving outcomes these children are showing.

Talk boxes

There is nothing mysterious about a 'talk box'. It is exactly what it sounds like: a box to promote talk. Talk boxes can come in any shape or size. Sometimes you might want the children to talk about the box, sometimes its contents, or sometimes both. It is worth building up a collection of boxes, from tiny to huge and made from a variety of different materials. The more interesting the clasp or fastenings, the better. Talk boxes are not restricted to small boxes. You can get some great talk in a large cardboard box.

What you put in your talk box is only really limited by your imagination. The only rule is that it contains things that children are going to want to talk about – nothing dull or mundane! When I use talk boxes I will sometimes put in unusual objects that the children may not have seen before, things that they can touch and feel. If you want children to talk, then you have to give them something to talk about. I find that the best items for this are the ones that are unexpected, especially if they have an element of fright or gore! A beetle, a top set of dentures, a plastic severed finger, rotten fruit (all mushy and mouldy) are all great examples of what could go in the boxes … and the list goes on.

I once found a perfectly preserved dead bumble bee on a window sill. I put this into a small plain cardboard box. The initial reaction of the children when they opened it was usually fright, but this was followed by fascination. They were often full of stories about being stung by bees,

or they were keen to tell me what they knew about bees. There was never a lack of conversation. Even if they really didn't like the bee, we could talk about why. Then I would encourage them to touch the bee and feel how soft it was. Hold it in the palm of their hand and look at the hairs on its legs through a magnifying glass. At this point the use of talk and language would change and become more about questioning and observation than preference.

When the bee had been so well handled that a couple of legs had dropped off and it was going a bit bald from too much stroking, I removed its wings. I put the wings in a tiny glass bottle with a cork stopper and asked the children who the wings belonged to. It turns out they are fairy wings. Apparently, just like we get a first set of teeth that we lose when our adult teeth come through, fairies have a first set of wings that they 'shed' when their adult wings come through. You are VERY lucky if you happen to find some and I have got a full set!

As well as talk boxes, you can have 'shout boxes' and 'whisper boxes'. They would both have in them a piece of information that the finder would have to go and shout about or whisper about, both indoors and out (especially outside, if they are shouting).

If you have boxes that are big enough for a child to fit in to, you can cut a hole in their side and join them together with lengths of downspout cut to size. Children can then pass secret messages or just tell a good joke down the tube.

There are lots of boxes that you can buy that are made for you to record some talk into that will play back to the children as they open it. These can be useful if you want the children to engage in some specific talk about what is in the box. You can use the box to encourage the children to use questioning language or investigative language. Ask them to talk about particular features or properties of what they have found inside their box

Get them talking –
The Hampshire Project

Children's talk can be a product of a well-planned and enhanced learning environment; it can also help to shape how the learning environment looks, from the display on the walls to the provision on the shelves.

Good display in early years settings should help to raise children's attainment by reminding them of key learning, or raise their self-esteem by featuring not only the work that they produce but also what they say about it. Making children's voices a key part of your classroom or setting environment is not only necessary for child-led planning, it also highlights for children the link between talking and writing and, best of all, it lets them know that you thought what they said was important enough to write down for everyone to read.

Identifying children's preferences through their talk and using them to 'dress' your next steps planning for maximum engagement is crucial. If I asked you to talk me through the activities you had planned or the themes and topics you have chosen to teach, could you show me evidence of how they linked to something a child had said, to their preference? Or are they just the ones that you always do, because they are on the list.

In 2012 I was asked by Hampshire Local Authority to come and work with four of their settings which had been identified as having outstanding practice. The idea behind the project was to see where a setting could be taken when it was already performing at a high level. In the first group I had a private day nursery, a pack-away pre-school, a two-form entry Reception in an infant school and a two-form entry Reception in a primary school. This was going to be interesting.

There were many great ideas that came out of the project; but the two that were consistent throughout were the use of children's talk for learning in display and the use of children's talk to shape the environment and planning. There was no 'end point' with the project work. We just established a starting point and then set off on a journey of development and discovery.
(This is beginning to sound like a self-help book!)

Talking to children
(Noah's Ark Pre-School)

Noah's Ark is a pack-away pre-school that has ownership of one middle-sized store cupboard and a setting out and packing away procedure that rivals any tessellation game on the Krypton Factor. It is amazing what that team manage to get in and out of that cupboard. On my first visit they had set up fifteen areas indoors and as much outdoor provision as they could fit into their minimal outdoor space.

There are four key workers who set up, support, interact and teach, all under the watchful eye of Helen their leader and Angela their deputy. The area is one of significant social deprivation, and there is a large cultural mix in the local community which results in the team having a number of children for whom English is an additional language. Yet, Helen and her team do not see this as a barrier to success and they strive to support all children in high levels of independent learning. There are designated times of the session when the children meet with their Key Worker, but the rest of the time they have free access to the environment.

On my first visit to the setting I was very impressed with the level of independence that all of these children were showing in all of the areas that they were working in. When I quizzed Helen further about how the team taught the children to be so self sufficient, her answer was simply, 'Talk'. But on further observation I could see that it wasn't just any old talk. It was well-planned specific talk that was targeted at individual children and based on their next steps development.

When listening to the team talk to children what immediately struck me was that, alongside being really warm and friendly,

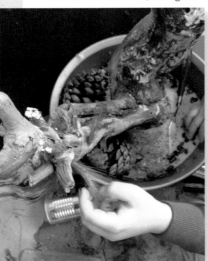

they all talked in the same way. By that I don't mean that they all had the same accent or a script, but it was clear that there was a cohesive approach to all aspects of their interactions with children. When talking to the children they always made sure that they were at the children's eye level (this may sound obvious, but you would be amazed how often I see children with a crick in their neck, trying to talk to adults who are towering above them!).

When coaching children on how to use different areas of the environment their language was the same. It didn't matter who you were working with, you were going to get the same message. It also occurred to me that they spent more time listening than they did talking, and when they did speak what they said was clear relevant and to the point. I am beginning to make them sound like androids, but they are anything but. Their interactions were very natural and nurturing. As a result of this cohesive approach there was some impressive practice taking place which resulted in high achievement from all of their children.

It was at Noah's Ark that I saw my first ever free-flow snack with children of this age. It wasn't as if they were just helping

themselves to a piece of fruit, they were collecting their own pottery bowl and metal spoon, serving their own cereal and pouring their own milk from a glass jug. If they fancied a bit of toast, then they could help themselves to bread (which some of them would have made with an adult in the bread-maker the day before), put it in the toaster and wait for it to pop up. While they were waiting they went and got a pottery plate and a knife and, once the toast was done, they put it on their plate, took it to the table and buttered it.

While I watched all of this take place, I was the only adult in the snack area. These children were managing this space completely independently. One thing that really made me chuckle was the use of the 'bossy girl', which I think is more commonly referred to as peer tutoring! There were two girls in particular in the snack area who took it upon themselves to organize everyone else. What was funny (but very effective) was that you could hear the language of the staff coming out of their mouths as they routined the children who were less familiar with the process, or supported the children with English as an additional language. The high expectations didn't stop with making the snack – they had to clear up after themselves as well. This included a washing-up station, where the children emptied out any leftovers, washed, dried and put away their plates dishes and spoons.

Since there was a high expectation for independence and no intervening adults present, there was a need for the children to talk. An opportunity had been created to develop their talk on multiple levels. I saw talk for negotiation, sharing, compromise, conflict resolution, turn taking, stating a preference, as well as a good old gossip over their toast and jam!

Other areas of the provision had not just been set out for high-level engagement; they had been created with the specific focus of creating opportunities for talking and sharing. The paint areas had a large easel that the children could share, either on a collaborative piece of work or individual pieces side by side.

The paint is not ready-mixed and all of the children mix their own from powder, often using a shade card. The process of mixing the paint itself is one that promotes language and discussion about texture, colour and cause and effect.

There are lots of interesting objects for the children to look at and touch, to encourage them to ask questions about what they might be or how they might be used.

Activities like the sawing of the wood and the deconstructing of the printer are not only good for developing fine- and gross-motor skills but they are also brilliant for facilitating high-level engagement and a range of talk topics including, 'What would happen if I sawed my finger off?'!

Originally the small-world resources were grouped in large boxes and the children had to spend a lot of time digging through the box to find what they wanted and see what was in there. Helen and the team felt that this was getting in the way of the actual small-world play and the children's talk development, so they now create a selection of clearly visible small-world groups on the shelves. This means that they children can easily see what is available, make a more informed choice and their play can start immediately.

The small-world area used to have one large and rather busily patterned rug in it. The rug has now been removed and the children can select from a variety of mats and rugs in different sizes, shapes and textures. These promote talk for preference and reasons for choice and also allow more than one type of small-world play to happen in the area at any one time.

Helen and the team have replaced all of their generic labelling with personalized ones, featuring the current cohort engaged in demonstrating appropriate use of a resource or area. This has not only raised the level of engagement within the areas but also given the children a sense of input to that particular space which the team are using as the starting point for peer tutoring.

All of the cupboards that Noah's Ark use have to be fold-away and/or collapsible. As space is of a premium they try and use the cupboard tops as part of their storage for continuous provision or an area for display. There was one particular cupboard top which is just at child height and nice and long and thin. No matter what the team put on it, it always ended up on the floor and the cupboard top was turned into a road. When I last visited the setting the cupboard top had been cleared and the road had become a permanent feature, When I asked Helen what had brought this about, she said that it eventually occurred to the staff that no matter what they did the children had different ideas for this space; so rather than fight against it, they asked them what they would like it to be. The unanimous decision was that it should be a road for cars and so that is what it has become. Sometimes it is easy to miss what children are clearly telling you, and an opportunity to articulate their thoughts and feeling is all it needs.

I have made three visits to Noah's Ark over the period of about a year. During that time some children have come and gone and some of the team has changed. Despite these disruptions the children have made brilliant progress, particularly in their talk and levels of independence. Helen and her team who really understand the importance and value of quality talk, have created a positive culture and consistent practice that focuses on accurate small-steps assessment and high-quality learning opportunities which in turn promote very successful learning. How do the team manage to achieve this? I hear you ask. By talking to each other constantly of course!

Children's talk to show their learning
(Crofton Hammond Infant School)

Lots of the children at Crofton Hammond Infant School had lots to say about themselves and their learning. What they talked about and how they talked about it was a really powerful illustration of what they were learning, how they felt about their learning and the impact that it was having on their attainment. But, to get all of that useful information you had to first catch yourself a child and then grill them! One of the focuses of my project work here was to utilise the children's talk in a variety of ways throughout the setting to show interest, engagement and attainment.

Crofton Hammond is a two-form entry infant school. There are 60 children in Reception, two teaching staff and two support staff. I was working, with Jodie one of the Reception teachers. All 60 children share one space which has two large areas connected by a longer, thinner area (a bit wider than a corridor – but not much). Each class starts its day on its own carpet space with the teacher; then they have free access to the provision. The six areas are spread across the whole space.

The staff have done a lot with the space that they have got. They were constantly re-evaluating how it was being used and moving or 'tweaking' their provision to meet the needs they identified. The environment was very welcoming and full of well thought-out, well coordinated display that gave great impact when you walked in, and had clearly taken a lot of thought and effort.

Even though the environment had visual impact what I thought it lacked was the children's voice. I could see lots of information about key words, colours, days of the week, months of the year, but not a great deal about what the children's learning preferences were, how their thoughts and feelings were recorded and how this influenced planning and teaching. As I observed the day unfold, I could see that the relationships between staff and children were brilliant and that the children's talk was very much valued. The mission became to show how the children's voices shaped learning through display, and how listening and valuing their talk shaped the learning experiences they were offered.

Following my first visit Jodie created her list of action points. They were:

- Clearly displayed individual and group learning.

- To value children's individual learning and voice in display in the same way that it is done in their learning journeys.

- Use children's talk through display to record how learning is differentiated and skill based.

- Use children's talk in display to show quantifiable attainment.

It was decided to use a 'scrap book' approach to some of the display to achieve these aims.

This is where the display is created as the theme or interest is developed. The display has many diverse elements to it which is why it is called a 'scrap book'. Assessment tells practitioners what it is that the children need to learn next; but how that learning is presented or 'dressed' is dictated by the children's preferences and interests. This process is recorded as part of the display.

Jodie also wanted to pilot the idea of an individual learning wall where children's individual achievements would be displayed with some annotation from both children and staff. The focus for this display was going to be around the workshop area. To do this she split two of her main display boards into equal sections. Each section would then display a piece of work created by an individual (or more if the piece was collaborative). The child's photograph would be displayed alongside their masterpiece with a comment from them and an observation from an adult.

A true scrap book display for me is not something that you can really plan in advance. The whole essence of it is that is born out of an area of children's interest, not something that you have necessarily planned for next half-term. What you are looking out for is anything that gives you really high-level engagement from a lot of children and then you run with that see how it goes.

Jodie's first scrap book display came about as the result of a child's request for the story of 'The Three Little Pigs'. As is often the way with a well-read classic (read well by Mrs Archer on this occasion), there was lots of high-level engagement and interest. Rather than start a 'Three Little Pigs' topic and rush out to collect sticks, the team looked at the next steps assessment and planned which objectives they needed to teach next and prepared to 'dress' those objectives in the theme of the 'Three Little Pigs' for the children who were interested.

As you can see from the photographs, lots of children produced a variety of things, using a variety of skills from a variety of areas of the environment. Good adult intervention ensured that each child was carrying out that activity at a level that was challenging their skill development and taking them forward. This challenge and differentiation can be clearly seen by what is displayed and how that display is annotated with children's talk and adult comment.

Not all children were interested in 'The Three Little Pigs'. Someone even penned the 2012 version of 'The Princess and the Pea'! Diversity in display is a good thing as it shows that staff are valuing and responding to children's interest and high levels of engagement.

At the other end of the classroom another scrap book display was emerging, this time inspired by another book *Don't Let Aliens Get My Marvellous Mum!* by Gillian Shields and Liz Pichon. It not only produced lots of quality talk work but also served as a very engaging vehicle for the teaching of individual next steps objectives.

Meanwhile the workshop area had been moved from its old position in a smaller enclosed space to its new spot in one of the central areas. This way more children would see and be aware of the learning walls and be inspired to get involved.

The individual sections clearly show how the interests of the children, supported by next steps planning from the adults, produce visible learning.

Such was the success of the learning walls in the workshop area that the principle was also transferred into mark making.

Jodie and her team were keen to really focus in on developing lots of different aspects of children's talk through the provision that they offered, rather than creating areas of learning and hope that talk happened. After a little persuasion they took a leap of faith and turned what had been their doctor's surgery into a deconstructed role-play area with some great results. One of the things that was really noticeable was the diversity of talk experiences that were now readily available, depending on the children's interests and needs.

Enhancement boxes full of props were still provided and adults used them in direct teaching. But when the children were in continuous provision, their imagination was their only restriction.

The final focus of the project was to look at how Jodie could use children's talk about their personal preferences to impact directly on to general and specific aspects of attainment. Jodie's continuous provision was well stocked and easily accessible; but one of the problems that she was having was that children tended to choose low-level non-challenging tasks, unless prompted by an adult to do otherwise. What we set out to do was to use the subjects that they talked about most to 'dress' some of the provision that was put out.

It is important to recognize that this is not about gender preferences, but individual preferences. Having said that, there are likely to be some areas – especially to do with popular culture – that are predominantly favoured by the same gender.

In the mark-making area a large group of children expressed an interest in Ben 10 and Superheros and another significant group in Dora the Explorer and all things Disney Princess. As a result two boxes were created that were dressed to the requested themes and filled with resources that were likely to move learning forward of the children who had expressed an interest.

For very specific intervention, we introduced the use of 'challenge bags'. These bags were themed around the interests of particular children and created individually for them. The bags are named and it is clear to the child which adult in the setting they need to communicate with regarding the contents of their bag.

In the photos there are two examples of the type of challenge bag they used. Amelie's is themed around her favourite thing – princesses and Joshua's around Lightning McQueen. The purpose of these bags was to tackle particular issues that both of these children were having with letter formation, but they can be used for any purpose whatsoever.

During my visits to Crofton Hammond I saw a noticeable change in the content of the display in Jodie's room. It was just as vibrant as it was on my first; but now it gave a much clearer picture of engagement, attainment and was a more accurate reflection of the hard work and commitment of the whole team. You could walk into the space and look at the display and see diversity, differentiation, a wealth of experiences, children's voice, adult assessment, child-led learning, skills-based teaching, and all without picking up a planning file or speaking to an adult or a child. The environment really did tell a very detailed learning story.

An environment for talk
(Little 1's)

In a private day nursery you will often have children from birth to four years old (and older if they run before and after school provision). If ever there was a good place to see all of the stages of language development then this is it. Little 1's had taken the unique approach of having mixed age provision that really allowed for high level peer tutoring and family support. What I wanted to help them to do was to ensure that their environment was structured in a way that supported talk development in a mixed age group.

Amey works at Little 1's day nursery and is one of Hampshire's Leading Foundation Stage Practitioners. Amey had been asked to be part of the project as Little 1's had been really examining the effectiveness of their practice and making some big changes to the 'usual' way in which day nurseries are run to bring them in line with more current and up-to-date thinking. The biggest change they made was to move from having lots of individual rooms for ages and stages of development to the concept of 'family grouping'.

Amey and the team soon realise that this shift wasn't going to be a purely cosmetic one. It had ramifications for the aspect of their nursery, including staffing, training, environment and parents and carers. Job roles and key responsibilities had to be changed and the environment was going to have to serve a whole new purpose.

After lots of hard work, the team established the basic principles and environment to be able to run a family-grouping nursery. There were no stair gates; there was complete free flow indoors and outdoors for all ages, and only a two-way split in the nursery.

They created a 'Nest' for 0 to 3 years and 'Pre-school' for 2 years to rising 5 years. There was no longer a magic 'It's your birthday – off you go to another room.' They aimed to allow the children to have the longest relationship with their key person possible. Some staff even requested to move room because they wanted to stay with the children and their families. Parents were also given a great deal of say on the transition period too.

The team at Little 1's had worked extremely hard to get the best provision possible in place. They had taken an original concept, listened to the ideas and views of staff and parents to ensure that everyone was clear with the vision and understood the basic pedagogy. Now that they had that in

place, they wanted to ensure that they used children's voices to create an environment that maximized the potential for quality learning and quality talk.

Little 1's was warm welcoming and full of bright display. Staff had clearly spent a lot of time and effort creating material and laminating and displaying it. But, other than looking attractive, it told me very little about the practice in the setting or the learning experiences that the children were having.

So, the first ABC exercise we did was a 'Why is it there, who is it there for and whose idea was it?' audit of the environment. For someone who is not connected emotionally with a setting, this is a really useful and painless process to go through; but it can be significantly more unnerving when you have put your heart and soul into creating your environment. I am really pleased to say that Amey handled it brilliantly and, although I could see there were moments when she looked more than a little crestfallen, she could see the sense in what we were doing and that made it a worthwhile exercise.

There was lots about the provision that made good sense, but it still seemed to be very focused around adult-led topics and themes and there wasn't a great deal of evidence of children leading their learning.

After my initial visit Amey and the whole team completed an 'environment audit' using the 'Why is it there, who is it there for and whose idea was it?' approach.

Then they used that audit as an action plan to begin to change the environment in order to enhance talk for children and to reflect children's talk. They really had to fight the temptation to do everything at once. As soon as they could see what they wanted to do and how they could do it, then they just wanted it done. But, it is the same with adults as it is with children. Too much too soon can do more damage than good. So make a plan and stick to it!

The first point on the action plan was to tackle the display and this was a 'quick win' and easy to do. If there was anything way above child height or irrelevant to children's learning, however pretty, it was taken down and replaced with a display featuring the children and the learning process.

Part of the strategy developing children's talk was to increase the level of independent access to resources so that children could make personal choices rather than just use what they had been given. Resources were moved to positions where they could be easily accessed.

Children were coached in how to access their own resources in the paint and snack areas. They began to confidently and competently do the tasks that they would previously have had to be with an adult to do.

Child-led themes became the focus of the main displays with lots of evidence of the diversity of skills that could be covered whilst running with children's ideas.

The team were looking carefully at all of the stages of development across all of the areas of learning, ensuring that they were catering for all ability levels and skill levels across their mixed age groupings. Part of the focus of this project was to take what had been identified by assessment that needed to be taught and dress those objectives in activities that reflected children's learning styles, personal and cultural preferences.

A display was then created using these images as a visual 'memory jogger' for the children about the skills that they had just learnt.

The children at Little 1's had always had the opportunity to engage in a wide range of experiential activities, but the focus on developing types of talk in children meant that these activities were now more closely associated with different levels of talk development and therefore could be used more strategically.

The kitchen role-play area was maintained as a familiar base for emergent language development, but the space was significantly enhanced with a deconstructed role-play to promote the use of many different types of talk as well as higher order problem-solving skills and sustained shared thinking. Engagement in the deconstructed role-play was high, so lots of other learning opportunities were introduced alongside it to maximise on that engagement.

There is not really an end point for this project at Little 1's. It will carry on long after my direct input has ended. The quality of the provision in the

setting was always good and the staff were forward thinking and completely focused on the best outcomes for the children. From my point of view, the impact of the project has just been to streamline their thinking and to bring the environment in line with the pedagogy for learning that underpins their ethos.

I asked Amey if she could sum up the project, which was a struggle for her as she is not the type of talker who finds 'succinct summing up' easy. She said: 'We have been reminded to look at our environment through the eyes of a child and use their voices to shape the content of what we put in it.' Couldn't have said it better!

Talk for attainment
(St Thomas More's)

It is undoubtedly true that high level engagement results in high level attainment. Getting that high level engagement and then using it to maximum impact is the key. In Reception at St Thomas More's Catholic Primary School we were looking a how we could us the children's interests to lead the planning and how we could then show the impact of that process through display.

When you walk into Tim's classroom it has certainly got the 'WOW' factor. He is a man with an eye for display. There was lots going on around his room which was very well coordinated, but the one thing that struck me about it was that, although Tim clearly had a really good understanding of his children's needs and achieved a high level of engagement with all of the children in his class, there was little evidence of this in his environment. Much of the display was computer generated from a selection of download sites. What I wanted Tim to do was to keep the 'feel' of his room but personalize it far more to his children, to heighten their interest and raise engagement which would then impact on attainment.

Once I was long gone after my initial visit, Tim fed back to his team lots of the things that we had discussed. Although they were positive on the whole, it is quite understandable that there were some questions about what it was all about and why a school that got good results needed to change their practice.

I think one of the key findings of this bit of the project was that it is important to try and find a mechanism to involve the whole team in some sort of discussion on the first visit so that everyone has the opportunity to discuss the points for development. I know this is not always possible, due to time and finding bodies/funding to allow release, but it should definitely be high on the priority list.

Even though Tim managed to do a great deal in a very short space of time, he was very sensible about the size of the initial changes he was going to make. Although he was tempted to take loads of material down and start again, he focused on a couple of key areas where he thought a personalized display would have the most impact. This also gave the rest of his team a chance to get their heads around what he was trying to achieve and to see its impact for themselves.

Tim had taken the concept of a personalized alphabet and run with it! The child's picture was the starting point, if their name started with that sound (not just letter), and then the children made a collection of other objects that also started with that sound.

In the parallel class to Tim, the team had created a personalized number line with the children. This had to be strung from the ceiling because of the current layout of the room, but that will not be its permanent home. As soon as space is made available, it is moving to child height for maximum impact.

To encourage the use of the outdoor equipment and other areas of the classroom, the team had cut photographs out from the catalogue that the equipment was ordered from. Tim replaced these with photos of children in the setting using the equipment.

When Tim and I were first discussing the idea of personalizing the learning environment, I showed him a photograph of a great piece of display that I had seen used by Vanessa at St Philips C of E Primary in Salford in order to engage parents. Vanessa's idea was that she took a 'learning story' and wrote it out like a story that would be really easy for non-educationalists to access. Then alongside the 'story' she wrote about the skills that the child would have covered during the activity and what the practitioners were going to do next to take that forward.

These learning stories can also be copied and used in children's learning journeys.

This is Tim's version of the 'learning story'. As the subject in question is a real animal, as opposed to a fictional one, he has presented it with lots of the features of a non-fiction text. Not only does it raise children's self-esteem by being up on the wall, it also shows a good example of children's interests shaping the curriculum and inspires others to have a go.

One of the things I had been looking at with Tim was the role of the adult during continuous provision. Each of the adults working in CP also had a planned objective that they have differentiated and then deliver as and when it is appropriate. Sometimes there is no activity planned and the adult take the objective into play and sometimes there is a 'starter' activity for interest and engagement.

This is a KUW objective with a dead fish starter. It never fails to engage!

We had also looked at what particular aspects of outdoor play make it different to play indoors Tim and the team are now clear on what skills their outdoor play is promoting, like this large-scale water play.

Inside, there was some great work with challenge bags being used to target individual children. Not only was their challenge linked to current assessment but it was also dressed to their particular interests. Talking pegs were used to remind the children what they needed to do (see photo on previous page).

If all of that wasn't enough to focus on, Tim had also looked at personalizing his display for impact on learning. This is a number assessment using foam-disc firing guns. There were two scrapbook displays in the setting. The first featured a learning story that was started by Freya and Faye. They canvassed the rest of the class for 'snack preferences'; they created a shopping list, went to the shops and bought what was needed; they washed it, chopped it and it was eaten!

The other learning story came from a child who shared with the class that she went to ballet. This sparked a lot of interest and a theme was born! The children ended up watching a performance of The Nutcracker!

Tim's original 'dayglow' wall that featured 30 versions of the same Elmer when I first visited is now long gone. It has been replaced by a wall of pride where children display their own chosen piece of work. Each square has the child's comments about what they have produced and why they have chosen it as well as an adult comment and next steps. This time it is the work that is the feature and not the backing!

It was really easy to see children's voice, skill development, diversity and adult knowledge of assessment and next steps, just by looking at the walls.

It has been a pleasure to work with Tim and to share his ideas and enthusiasm over the past year. It was great to visit him at the end of an academic year and see his wall absolutely dripping with evidence of high-level engagement and high-level attainment. Having said that, Tim said that he feels the project is far from over. Apparently there is a key word display made out of a download of laminated house bricks that he is itching to take down and replace with something a bit more child friendly! I look forward to seeing it!

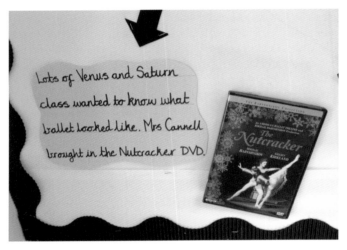